STEPPARENT

IS NOT A BAD WORD

DAVID Z. NOWELL, Ph.D.

Publishers Since 1798

THOMAS NELSON PUBLISHERS

Nashville

Published in Nashville, Tennessee, by Thomas Nelson, Inc., Publishers, and distributed in Canada by Word Communications, Ltd., Richmond, British Columbia, and in the United Kingdom by Word (UK), Ltd., Milton Keynes, England.

Unless otherwise noted, Scripture quotations are from THE NEW KING JAMES VERSION of the Bible. Copyright © 1979, 1980, 1982, Thomas Nelson, Inc., Publishers.

Scripture quotations noted KJV are from The Holy Bible, KING JAMES VERSION.

Scripture quotations noted RSV are from the REVISED STANDARD VERSION of the Bible. Copyright © 1946, 1952, 1971, 1973 by the Division of Christian Education of the National Council of the Churches of Christ in the U.S.A. Used by permission.

Library of Congress Cataloging-in-Publication Data
Nowell, David Z.
  Stepparent is not a bad word : advice and perspectives for parenting your stepchildren / David Z. Nowell.
      p.   cm.
  Includes bibliographical references.
  ISBN 0-7852-8279-3
  1. Stepparents. 2. Stepchildren. 3. Stepfamilies. 4. Family-Religious life. I. Title.
HQ759.92.N69 1994
306.874—dc20   93-37445
                                                          CIP

Printed in the United States of America
1 2 3 4 5 6 7 - 00 99 98 97 96 95 94

CONTENTS

Author's Preface

This is a book born of personal necessity. In 1990, I married a woman with two young daughters. As my wife and I began to encounter the situations and events that are the reality of life in the stephome, we made our way to the bookstores and libraries in search of perspectives and answers. There we found sociological treatises, statistical studies, self-help psychology tracts, and legal analyses.

But our home is a Christian home, and we were looking for an approach to life's questions that came from a specifically Christian perspective. What we discovered, however, was a surprising absence of material. The few authors who addressed stepfamily relationships did so in one of two ways. Some wrote of stepfamily issues as a subsection of a larger discussion of the Christian home. Others focused primarily on the dynamics of the blended family, which is but one type of stepfamily. In our case, I had no children with whom to "blend" my stepfamily. We simply did not find the material we needed.

But why a book on the Christian stepfamily? Because stepfamilies face challenges that traditional families will never encounter. But why *Christian* stepfamilies? Because stepfamilies occur at about the same percentage in the church as they do in society as a whole, and they need the ministry and ministry opportunities that come only within the context of the Christian faith.

Unfortunately, however, the teaching, the programs, and the ministry of the church largely focus on the traditional two-parent biological family. For example, how many churches plan children's activities on Sunday afternoon before the evening service, even though most stepchildren are returning to their homes following weekend visitation? Many stepchildren cannot participate in children's choir or missions programs because of such scheduling. When the church does plan for the stepfamily, it is usually in the form of a special program designed to deal with the stepfamily as an aberration.

Therefore, this book offers a perspective on the stepfamily with an explicitly Christian agenda. The stepfamily is seen as God's provision in a broken world. It is a venue for ministry. It is the promise that God will meet our needs wherever he finds us.

A few notes on method and procedure are in order here. First, some chapters seem to be permeated by a negative tone. Such a tone is a result of open discussion of the problems unique to the stepfamily. I have tried to address these problems and offer answers and perspectives for them. In each case, I have tried to present the positive side as well as the potential for growth and ministry in even the most difficult situations.

In the stepfamily, Romans 8:28 must be more than a promise; it is a living reality.

Second, one of the more difficult tasks involved the question of gender-exclusive language. When we are discussing lives of persons, there is simply no useful gender-exclusive pronoun to employ. Therefore, I have attempted to be balanced in the use of male and female designations, all the while attempting to preserve the flow of the written language. I hope that I have been at least somewhat successful in the task.

Finally, this book focuses specifically on the stepfamily that exists because of divorce and remarriage. While I am fully aware that stepfamilies may also be brought into being by the death of a parent, coherence in approach demanded that I limit the scope of this discussion. The challenges and triumphs of the stepfamily in which the child still has two living biological parents are very different from those in which a parent has died. This focus is by no means an ignoring or denigration of the other form, but only a recognition and limiting of a task.

This is a work of personal experience, an outgrowth of the challenges and blessings of my own family. Therefore, I am especially grateful to my wife, Susan, and my stepdaughters, Jinnifer and Meredith. Their perspectives, insights, and response to these pages were invaluable.

This manuscript was by no means a one-person effort. Susan not only reviewed drafts, but also typed, edited, and proofed. Milton Cunningham and Jarrell McCracken supported the project and forwarded the manuscript to the publisher. All the good folks at

Thomas Nelson, from vice presidents to editors to author liaisons, were sources of constant encouragement and help. To all of these, I offer a heartfelt "Thank you."

David Z. Nowell
July 1993

CHAPTER ONE

What Are We Doing Here Anyway?

God instructs the heart not by ideas, but by
pain and contradictions.
    —Jean Pierre De Caussade

This was not in the equation when you planned
your life. The formula was simple: finish high school,
probably college, find someone with whom you share
values, interests, and commitments; marry, spend a year
or two growing together, and then start a family—a
family that was completely self-contained. There would
be, certainly, other influences, other voices to which your
family would respond: grandparents, church, school,
friends, and larger community, but you and your spouse
would solely determine (with some direction from
above) the path down which your children would walk.

Nice dream. Now welcome to the reality. The children with whom you share your home are not biologi-
cally your own. They might not have known you for a
significant percentage of their lives. Though you provide them with their material needs, make physical and

emotional sacrifices for them, and bend over backward to make your habitation a home, they don't even call you "Mom" or "Dad." You did not realize that this was what "first-name basis" meant. You are a stepparent, and since you are reading this book, we can probably assume that you are also a Christian.

The Christian stepparent. The Christian stepparent? It's not an oxymoron—a contradiction in terms—anymore. For nineteen hundred and fifty years, a stepparent was someone who replaced a deceased parent; in 1900 over 90 percent of stepchildren had lost a parent to death. By 1970, that figure was down to 30 percent. Since the revolution in societal mores in the seventies, all but a fraction of stepchildren are from families of divorce and remarriage. The stepparent is now—almost exclusively— one who has married a divorced person with children. The contemporary stepparent is not re-creating a nuclear family but participating in the conception of a *bi*nuclear family, with at least three parental figures and multiple sibling roles.

This type of relationship has scarcely been addressed by the Christian community, because divorce did not happen in good Christian families—or if it did, its reality was ignored by the community of faith. But that is not the case anymore. Divorce and remarriage are as much a reality within the Christian community as among non-believers, as the statistics in a few pages will show. And this reality has its own special set of circumstances, challenges, and opportunities. It even has its own vocabulary: blended families, visitation rights, six-month splits.

No, this is not what you had planned, and, if you are

truthful, this is not God's ultimate design either. The Bible is quite clear that his intent is for wife and husband to remain committed and faithful to each other throughout their lives. Within the context of that commitment, children are to be brought into this world and raised up "in the ways of God."

But the Bible is equally clear that God is bigger than the circumstances of our lives, and, within our incompleteness, he can form something new and quite valuable. God can take the "steps" and make them into family. Perhaps a family with its own unique set of challenges, but also a family that God may uniquely bless—and a family that may see its children grow to become faithful and loving children of God.

Your Spouse's Children: Choosing Relationships and Accepting Situations

This is a book of affirmations. It is a study of positives. It's about old-fashioned values in contemporary society. It's about softball games, school pictures, proms, and family vacations. It is about late night talks, midnight cries, and driver's education. It is about church picnics, summer camp, and graduation. It is about all the things that make a family *a family*. It is also about the unique challenges and privileges of the family that God has brought together in his special ways. If you are a stepparent, you have almost certainly found yourself in a relationship of your choice that brings about situations in which you had no choice. And that relationship and those situations are precisely what this book addresses.

Hopefully, you and your husband or wife entered into

your relationship advisedly—with your eyes open. You understood that the choice to initiate a relationship was not a choice you were making solely for yourselves and for the future in-laws, but also for your spouse's children and—ultimately—the exes, former in-laws, and even the ex's new husband or wife. We will call this last group the "extended relationships." It is very often these relationships that most severely test your parenting ability. The extended relationships may even prove to be the ultimate measure of the depth and strength of your relationship with your mate.

When Susan and I married, we did not exchange vows only with each other. Instead, her (now *our*) daughters stood with us, and we became not just husband and wife, but *family*. Of a certainty, we designed the marriage ceremony as we did for the benefit of the girls, to make them understand that they were an integral part of our relationship, but that was not the exclusive reason. I wanted Jinnifer and Meredith to be a part of the ceremony so that, when those "I didn't ask for this!" days arrived, I would always remember that I knew what I was getting into. I can't plead ignorance.

What I did *not* do was exchange vows with my wife's former family. I talked to one young woman who had recently married a man with two small boys. After a particularly exasperating time in the relationship, she exclaimed, "I did not know I was marrying his ex-wife, too!" But she was, and ultimately it is these tag-along relationships that perhaps fashion our parenting style as much as the relationships of choice. And, as we remember from high school algebra, the more factors we add to an equation, the more difficult it is to discern the answer.

It is something like watching a juggler. Just about anyone can "juggle" two balls. It takes but a modicum of talent to handle three or even four. But add five, six, or seven balls, and the talent gets impressive. If you add multiple and varied objects (a torch, an old boot, an ax, a chain saw), it really gets interesting. That is why the Flying Karamazov Brothers are world famous.

In the same manner, it is one thing to develop and nurture a relationship with your spouse and your children. It is quite another to have meaningful and worthwhile interaction with all the extended relations. Precisely that interaction is often mandated, however, for the well-being of the children, and it is in this very variety of relationships that God can work to create new venues of ministry, new paths of growth. The challenges there encountered may appear to be hindrances to parenthood, but they are also opportunities for the movement of God's hand. While the transitions are not always as smooth or harmonious as we might desire, the very dissonance makes it interesting. After all, no one pays to see a one-ball juggler.

The World in Which We Live

In the ideal Christian society, children would grow to adulthood in a caring environment with both biological parents. That ideal is simply not the reality American children experience each day. Only by moving our focus from the desired ideal and addressing the present reality may we provide for these children. Divorce is a widely prevalent expression of the dysfunctionalism which marks our world. One half of all marriages in the United States now end in divorce. Failure at the first effort, however, discourages few from remarriage. Unfortunately, statistics on divorce in second marriages indicate to us that most persons learn very little from the failure of their initial unions, bringing the same destructive personality traits, problem areas, and beliefs to their subsequent marriage(s).

The presence of children does not significantly decrease the likelihood of remarriage. When divorced persons remarry, their children—often with little voice in the matter—are swept into new familial relations. *It is estimated that as many as 1,500 children acquire stepparents every day.* Some ten million children are now stepchildren. Most of these children live with their mother and stepfather, because mothers retain custody of children in the vast majority of cases.

Stepfamilies fall into a variety of categories. In some stepfamilies, only one partner has been married; in others, both. In some, only one partner brings children of his or her own; others find both husband and wife bringing children from previous relationships. Almost one quarter of stepchildren live in homes with stepsiblings. In some American stepfamilies, the lines of relationships and extended relationships get unbelievably complex, as one or both partners bring children from multiple antecedent relationships and then see children born into the mix.

Tragically, the Christian community is not immune to this phenomenon. We do not exercise the practice of lifelong monogamy much better than the surrounding society. Such was not always the case. Divorce was taboo for so many years (and for centuries even outlawed) in the church. My father, a southern rural pastor and a man I mark as among the most compassionate I have ever known, for many years would not conduct a marriage ceremony if one of the partners was divorced. He held a deep conviction that to do so was to risk condoning adultery. I remember seeing him agonize over telling a cherished friend that he would not preside at her wedding. But for most of his life, churches were by and large rendered impotent when it was time to offer support for those experiencing divorce or remarriage.

Fortunately, the church evidences a growing recognition of the family of today. While many families do reflect the scriptural ideal, we are finally addressing the reality that many families are no longer constructed of their original parts. We are recognizing that millions of children who were on the cradle rolls in Sunday school have suffered through their parents' divorce and then experienced their remarriage. We are yet to provide, however, the answers and resources to ensure that the parents and stepparents in these reconstituted families are equipped to provide Christian guidance, nurture, and environment for their children.

Divine Omnicompetence

Perhaps the church can become more effective at addressing the needs of stepfamilies when we get a clearer picture of the God who can bless these unions. Theologians like to toss *omni-* words around when they talk about God: *omnipotence, omniscience, omnipresence.* Most of us find these words hard to really understand. What exactly does it mean to be all-powerful, all-knowing, and always present? We may confess these as attributes of God, but we are not sure exactly how they apply to our day-to-day life.

Let me introduce you to another *omni-* word—one that speaks immediately to our lives. The word is *omnicompetence.* Perhaps we can describe this divine attribute as God's ability to handle any situation that arises. Scripture is a record of divine omnicompetence. Time and time again God's people throw him a curve; they step outside his ideal for them. And time and time again, God takes the broken pieces and restores them into *his* new plan for them.

Spend a few hours reading the first two books of the Bible. In the initial chapters of Genesis we find the first evidence of how God relates to his people. In the Garden, God had a design for Adam and Eve—a design based on relationship. Adam and Eve chose to step outside that design. In making that choice they changed not only the way in which they would relate to God and each other, but also the very nature of God's relationship to all people. Their choice had consequence beyond themselves. That is not, however, the ultimate focus of the story, for the story of the Fall is not a story of destroyed relationship, but the proclamation of God's *provision* within our weakness. In fact, perhaps we really should refer to this as the story of the Provision rather than the Fall.

As you continue to read, however, notice how the cycle repeats itself. God designs a plan for his people; his people choose to step outside the relationship he has ordained; they recognize the price of their sin; God establishes a new provision. The new covenant God establishes is never God's original intent or will, but it always becomes his will in the arena of our fallenness. Even the greatest gift of all—the coming in human form of his Son—was a provision for fallenness. Though they are new, these provisions of God are no less his divine will than was the original relationship in the Garden.

So must it be in his provision for the reconstructed family. Divorce is not the divine intent. When a marriage is ended, God's intent for a family has been violated. That violation has repercussions not only for the principals, but also for the secondary and even tertiary relationships. Perhaps the children feel the effects of a divorce even more than do the parents. But even in the midst of the brokenness, God can create something new and very valuable. The new situation is not beyond his competence. And when God creates the new, the very best that this new can be becomes God's will for the recreated relationship. It is not his original intent, but it is no less his will. And you, as the new mate and the new parent, can be the agent of God's redemption.

Creating the New Out of Broken Pieces

Perhaps even more telling than the story of the Garden for the question at hand is the story of David and Bathsheba. Bathsheba was the wife of a warrior named Uriah the Hittite. From the roof of his palace one evening, David saw Bathsheba bathing. Desiring her, and knowing that her husband was off at war, David had an illicit relationship with Bathsheba. After some time passed, David received word that Bathsheba was pregnant. Eventually, David had Uriah killed in battle and took Bathsheba as a wife in order to hide their sin. David was confronted with his sin by the prophet Nathan. Soon after, Bathsheba gave birth to a son who died a few days after birth. David's lament and prayer for forgiveness became the beautiful and moving Fifty-first Psalm.

A relationship could not get off to a much more difficult start than that one. But God's provision far exceeded David's sin. David and Bathsheba had a second son whose name was Solomon, and he was king during Israel's greatest national period. Even given its sinful origin, God was able to use David's family to his glory.

These stories also teach us the importance of not getting sidetracked into an issue that is, at this point, largely extraneous and irrelevant: guilt carried from the ending of the child-producing relationship. Your spouse may hold varying levels of responsibility for the breakup of a previous relationship. There is a very significant chance that you yourself have experienced a failed marriage. The end of the previous relationships may have left scars (and we will deal with that extensively in a subsequent chapter), but you will not have success as a family until you forgive yourself and accept God's forgiveness.

If you or your spouse were at fault in a divorce (is there really such a thing as a no-fault divorce?), you need to seek forgiveness from the wronged parties—be they exes, former in-laws, or even your children. Then you must affirm that it is God's will, his divine plan, for your family to pick up the pieces and become what God has designed for you. You must not dwell on the failures of yesterday. We look back only to learn from our mistakes; we look forward to anticipate the movement of God's hand in our lives.

Throughout the ages, one of the affirmations of the church has been *creation ex nihilo;* that is, we believe that God created all that exists out of nothing. Closely related to this confession is the belief that whatever God has created, he will be active in redeeming. Indeed, if we understand redemption as God's continuing act of creation, it becomes the natural result of God's never-ending interaction with the world. We recognize that, if God is capable of creating all out of nothing, he is certainly able to reconstitute a new and worthwhile whole out of the pieces we present to him. The entirety of the gospel of the new covenant is a testimony that God does not quit on us despite our mistakes. As a friend remarked to Susan upon hearing of our engagement, "God can make the second time around better than the first."

There is one significant difference between the doctrine of *creation ex nihilo* and the doctrine of redemption. As he initially created, God acted alone. Conversely, the doctrine of redemption always calls for participation; for *our* own good, God wants us involved. While we affirm with Luther *sola gratia,* only by grace, we recognize that grace calls for response, a willingness to be God's instruments in redemption. Such willingness begins when we, like Hannah in the Old Testament, present our families to God, and then offer ourselves to be used of God to accomplish his purposes in our children's lives.

We never outgrow God's plan and direction in our lives. Your family may not be what you envisioned it to be nor what God initially construed it to be. But the promise of redemption is that God still desires the best for your family. What we must not do is put God in a box that prescribes how he will work in the new situation. We must give God the freedom to be God and to create something novel and valuable in our lives.

Why the Model Doesn't Work

Let's face it: the traditional family roles often cannot work in the stepfamily because of the dynamics of the new relationships. To be sure, it is much easier to work within a well-defined, rule-oriented structure—but that may not be the way God desires to work in your family.

When a new family is constituted, the members of that new family have undergone a number of changes—changes that, especially for the children, may evoke responses of confusion, apprehension, and even rebellion. First, the family has experienced a divorce, with its dissolution of familial roles. The father probably is no longer filling the role to which the children had grown accustomed. The mother may be assuming a role of authority which she has never before assumed. Additionally, both parents may be struggling with the new constructs of their life apart.

Perhaps before scars of this confusion have healed, another relationship is initiated. For the children brought into this new relationship, the confusion may be compounded. A new parental figure is introduced into the equation; perhaps there is a change of residence; perhaps new brothers and sisters enter their lives.

Perhaps the most difficult of the adjustments required by a new marriage is the demand of emotional immediacy. In the biological family, the children grow into relationship as they mature. Affection, house rules, turf adjustments, family taboos, and structures of authority all evolve and are constituted into the child's life at a relatively slow and even pace. Children cannot mark the moment when they first understand that they have mother and father, brother and sister, or when they were first required to love their family members, because such relationships have forever been a part of their environment.

Not so in the stepfamily. A child is introduced to a new parent and is expected immediately to embrace this person and to treat that person with all the respect and homage we feel is due the Christian parent. Factor in a stepbrother or stepsister or two, and it verges on being too much for the young mind to process. Who would not experience confusion and more than a little apprehension? A friend of mine paraphrases Kipling, "If you can keep your head when all those around you are losing theirs, then you have absolutely no grasp of the situation." Even when the child has positive expectations of the relationship, the reality of the new roles may demand difficult adjustments. The child may even be forced to deal with newly activated grief because the new marriage means that the dream of reuniting the parents has been crushed.

Remarriage *is* tough for children, and it is only nominally easier for the parent and stepparent. The first years of a marriage should be devoted to developing a relationship. That means that wife and husband should be learning each other, exploring personalities, and discovering roles. In the stepfamily, no such luxury is allowed. Husband and wife are expected to assume roles as soon as they return from their honeymoon. Energy that should be channeled toward construction of a stable and meaningful relationship is redirected toward the demands of parenting. In such a situation, we often want to revert to the familiar, to a standard set of operating rules for our family. Instead of letting relationships develop, we want to impose a preconceived structure of authority.

In our desire for rules, we revert to the oldest and most dangerous sin. Return for just a moment to the story of the Garden. What was at stake? The *relationship*. The writer of Genesis records that each evening Adam and Eve walked with God. Imagine that! It is the record of a very personal and intimate relationship. Adam and Eve, however, were simply not capable of living a lifestyle based on relationship. What did the tree offer them? Satan promised them that they would be like God, knowing good from evil. In other words, they would trade the relationship for information; right and wrong would be laid out for them. Their sin was their refusal to trust God in the manner that living in the tension of a relationship requires.

So it remains in our day. We desire rules more than relationships. Living in a relationship in which the rules are not hard and fast and the roles not externally imposed requires a large step of faith, both in God and in your mate. The difficult situation is exacerbated by the large number of contemporary prophets who tell us there is only one biblical model by which the family can be constituted. And thus, searching for the immediate and easy answer, we try to impose a structure on our family relationships which they are simply incapable of accepting.

Such an imposition may be the easier answer, but it may very well also be the worst of all choices. In the traditional answer, a family should be carefully constructed with the father as decision-making and spiritual head. The mother (submissive, of course!) is responsive to his leadership and instructs the children in ways of righteousness. The children, always well-scrubbed and polite, recognize that their parents are a gift from God, given them so that they may grow increasingly wise as they mature. It is caricature, of course, but we do often feel that to really be a *Christian* family, we must follow this master design.

The stepfamily is not, however, the traditionally constructed family. One of the most pervasive and dangerous myths of modern Christendom is that the stepfamily can become a rebuilt nuclear family. A traditional family structure may be as ill-fitting and painful for the stepfamily as wingtips on a mountain trail. If we are to be open and available to God to be used as he deems appropriate, we must be ready to step out of the traditional roles.

But what will replace those roles? I believe we begin with an open and honest assessment of what each spouse brings to the family relationship. Recognizing that God is God means that we allow him to use our particular talents *and unique set of circumstances* to act as he wills in the life of our family. In many stepfamilies, talents and abilities that were developed in previous relationships will serve the new family quite well. Business acumen, mechanical ability, teaching talent, or strength in financial planning is not gender-specific.

I have some very good friends who have recognized the importance of freedom in their family roles. The wife grew up on a west Texas ranch and was expected to help with the family chores just like her brother. The husband grew up in Dallas believing milk was produced at Kroger Foods. They have a beautiful rural home. There she makes the mechanical and maintenance choices; he runs the inside. And they have an exceptionally strong marriage. It takes all the talent that God assembles to make a family successful; we must not hinder his work by reserving certain tasks for male or female. We must give God the freedom to use us where he wills.

The roles to which our talents direct, however, must always be amended by the particular circumstance of the family itself. Take the question of discipline in the stepfamily, for example. There is no divine edict that places the man in charge of disciplining the children. Indeed, if the man is the stepfather, taking the role of disciplinarian as soon as the new family is brought into being can be absolutely disastrous for the newly formed relationships, especially if the children are older when the stepfather enters their lives. Instead, the new father, however good he may be as a disciplinarian, must first *earn* the respect of his new family. Even then, it may never work for him to be the primary figure for discipline in the family.

The bottom line is this: God is bigger than the categories in which we wish to place him. Therefore, his plan for your family may mean that you step outside your preconceptions of what a family ought to be. To do so means putting faith in the relationships (with God, with a spouse, with children) and faith in God's ability to work through relationships (with spouse, with children, with former mates and relatives) instead of in a set of rules. After all, only through relationships are we able to fulfill God's design for us.

CHAPTER TWO

Dealing with the Reality

That's not a problem. A problem is something you can do something about. What we have here is a fact of life.
—Milton Cunningham

When I was a small boy, my favorite day of the year was not Christmas or my birthday; rather, it was the day that the Sears Christmas Wish Book was delivered. On Christmas and my birthday, I had to face the reality that we were not a wealthy family and that the things most desired would probably never be seen. The day the Wish Book came, however, a young boy's fantasies became very real. I had telescopes and BB guns, race tracks and cars, footballs and helmets; nothing was beyond my reach. And I wanted it all.

The problem with the Wish Book was that it gave a false sense of reality. No matter what the family's financial position, the hope sprang eternal that, somehow, all those things could be mine. Then, when presents time rolled around, the reality could never measure up. No matter how great Santa's offerings, they could not match the dream world constructed in my fantasy. It took some years of growing to learn that enjoyment and meaningfulness in life demand that fantasy, the fervent desire that things be other than they are, be kept in proper perspective.

Unfortunately, the lesson is never synthesized in many stepfamilies. We have a picture of what we want our families to be; we construct a reality in our minds and spend our time wishing it were so or bemoaning the fact that it is not. We wish our children did not have to deal with having one parent attempt to manipulate the children's feelings by degrading the other parent. We wish we did not have to keep careful journals of our interaction with the other family. We wish our schedule were not interrupted by the children leaving every other weekend, or worse, that our precious time with the children amounted to more than a twice-monthly visit. The list could go on and on. And such desire becomes the focus of our existence.

We label these situations *problems,* and therein lies the *real* problem. My friend Milton Cunningham tells the story of meeting a man whose right arm was greatly malformed and of virtually no use. The man held out this arm and said, "Some people look at this arm and say that I have a problem. This arm is not a problem. A problem is something you can do something about. What we have here is a fact of life."

How many of the stepfamily's problems are actually facts of life? It is a distinction that we must all learn to make, because the approach to a problem is very different from the approach to a fact of life. We need to solve problems; we need to accommodate facts of life, all the while attempting to address the problems they spawn.

Mistaking facts of life for problems generates its own set of difficulties. Instead of constructive use of our energy, we spend our time damning and regretting the situation in which we live. More times than not, this problem initially affects the biological parent more than the stepparent. By and large, the stepparent had at least some idea of the situation when he or she walked into it. To be sure, we may all experience frustrating situations, but the chronic nature of unchanging situations is probably felt more intensely by the one who has been subject to the situation the longest.

For your spouse, the parent of your stepchildren, the challenges of reality are compounded by factors to which you may not be able to relate. You may not like the manner in which the other biological parent manipulates the children. You are not, however, dealing with the feeling that—through no fault of your own—someone is trying to turn your children against you. Neither are you dealing with feelings of anger which may remain from a bitter divorce. Therefore, the ugliness of the reality you face with your spouse may not be nearly so consuming for you.

Did you notice the phrase "through no fault of your own" in the preceding paragraph? We cannot fully address this issue of facing reality until we factor in the question of blame. While it is often stated that there is no such thing as a truly innocent party in divorce proceedings, we often find cases where one party genuinely has been victimized by the other. Even more important for you in your relationship with your spouse is the recognition that, no matter where the fault really lies, your spouse may feel that he or she has been victimized—if not in the breakup of the marriage, at least in the relationship with the children.

In a marriage where a husband has left his wife, she may rightly ask: "My marriage was destroyed. Why should I also be required to surrender my summer vacation with my children? I did not ask for any of this." The husband may respond, "I divorced you, not the children. Why should I always have to be the one who gives in?" Both sides are hurt, and both sides see victimization in their relationship with the children. The ending of the relationship between husband and wife may have been a voluntary choice for one or both of the partners, but that choice *imposed* a new reality upon the relationships with the children which almost certainly was not the preferred choice of either parent. It is not of their choice; it is a fact of life.

The facts-of-life reality can be generally subsumed into three large categories: 1) facts of life relating to the behavior or attitude of an ex-spouse, 2) facts of life regarding legal status of the relationship between parent and child, 3) facts of life that affect the well-being of the children. (We will address each of these areas in depth in subsequent chapters.) For virtually every parent legally estranged, separated, or divorced from the other parent of his or her children, each of these areas can be a constant source of difficulty and frustration. I have yet to meet a parent who has experienced a broken marriage who was completely satisfied with the status of any one of these areas. I have met many, though, who have discovered means of dealing with the reality of their situation.

Dealing with the reality, however, is not an arena reserved only for the parent. The realities imposed by the separation of biological parents will touch the whole of the existence of the family. It touches physical well-being, emotional life, spiritual walk, and—always—the newly formed relationships. Nothing is more central to your spouse's identity than the reality he or she faces which has been imposed by a previous child-producing relationship. Aside from the spiritual condition of the marriage partners, nothing is more the part and parcel of your relationship than those facts of life. You will face them every day for the rest of your marriage; they will always be a part of you.

The Same Boat

The most important lesson that the stepparent can learn is this: *You and your spouse are in it—all of it—together.* There is no such thing as her realm and his realm. You cannot impose such a division on your lives. What affects the parent also affects the stepparent. There is no such thing as "It's your problem, not mine" or, and this is equally important, "It's my problem, not yours."

Perhaps the first emotion experienced by the stepparent is the frustration of impotence to change parts of the reality imposed on the family. We desperately want to make things better for our families. In some situations, however, changes are beyond the realm of possibility. Inability to produce change can very quickly lead to frustration, which has potentially disastrous results for the psyche as well as the relationship. So it becomes

21

critically important to recognize the difference between a problem and a fact of life.

The frustration of not being able to produce change is compounded by the "rescue mentality" often brought into the relationship. When many of us who are now stepparents first began the courtship that would lead to marriage, we encountered a single parent who was, by and large, facing a seemingly hostile world alone. Our presence meant that this single parent had someone to shoulder part of the load, someone with whom to spend adult time, and someone to whom they could talk. That presence instantly made the life situation better—at times immeasurably better. If we are honest, that is probably part of the attraction for most of us; much of the fulfillment in the relationship came because we felt that we were vital to another's well-being.

The sense of purpose that is so fulfilling often leads us to link our worth in the relationship to our ability to make things better. To the question "What do you do in this relationship?" the answer is "I make things better." As long as "better" is defined as being a shoulder to cry on, standing beside your mate no matter the circumstance, or always letting your family know you care—the rescue mentality is kept under control and is generally positive.

When, however, the stepparent becomes so tied to that role in the relationship that he or she links relational success to the ability to repair or restore any situation, genuine difficulty is right around the corner. Many situations are simply beyond your purview. You cannot "fix" everything, and the attempt to do so can only lead to destructive frustration that precludes positive accommodation toward those "unchangeable" situations. You have seen the prayer that hangs in so many offices and kitchens, the one that ends "and the wisdom to know the difference." Perhaps the stepparent's prayer needs to be, "Lord, give me the wisdom to know the difference between a problem and a fact of life."

Play the Ball Where the Monkey Drops It

My friend Don Elliott has put together a wonderful little book called *Play the Ball Where the Monkey Drops It.* The feature lesson in this book is drawn from the Calcutta Country Club and Golf Course in Calcutta, India. Ground rule number ten on the golf course is, simply, "Play the ball where the monkey drops it." This ground rule may also provide a special insight for our families.

India itself is a country of contrasts. Though surrounded by slums of abject poverty, the Calcutta Country Club is one of the most posh and refined golf facilities in the world, reserved for the privileged few of wealth and affluence. This beautifully laid-out and maintained course is cut directly out of a magnolia jungle; thus, the course is surrounded by thick groves of huge, lush magnolias. These magnolias are also home to large monkey populations. In the trees, the monkeys find not only shelter from the sweltering Indian sun, but also a superb view of the fairways.

For reasons as yet undiscovered, these same monkeys have developed a special affinity for golf balls, especially as the balls bounce and roll toward the greens. As you might imagine, this affinity poses quite a problem for golfers. At the Calcutta Country Club, they have developed a unique solution to a unique problem.

23

As the golfer connects with the golf ball, a rustling can be heard among the magnolia trees. The ever vigilant monkeys spring from the trees in pursuit of the bouncing projectile. At that time, the caddie launches forth into his task: intimidating the monkeys. The caddie, madly waving a golf club, races down the fairway toward the ball. Usually these tactics succeed in preventing the monkey from capturing the ball. On occasion, however, the monkey is successful. As the monkey grasps the ball and flees, the caddie will intensify his efforts at intimidation. Invariably, at the approach of the human, the monkey will drop the golf ball. And there's the rub. The monkey may or may not drop the ball in the fairway, in a good lie, or even within the boundary. But the golfer is not allowed the prerogative of returning the ball to its original spot, regardless of whether its position has worsened or improved. Thus, we are left with the Calcutta Country Club Rule Number Ten: Play the ball where the monkey drops it.

When we begin to examine our lives as stepfamilies, we often discover that the courts or prior relationships have left us with "unfavorable lies." At that discovery, we are left with a choice: either we expend our lives trying to change the unchangeable and bemoaning our lot, or we deal with the reality. The first option can lead only to frustration; the second opens our lives to divine intervention that can make something meaningful and worthwhile out of that which has been broken.

Confronting Reality

There is a basic difference in the manner in which a problem is approached and the manner in which a fact of life is approached. We address problems by attempting to solve them, facts of life by structuring accommodation. To act differently toward either will always produce less than maximum results.

If problems are approached by accommodation, we are usually left to face that same problem again and again. I know of one father whose former wife and custodial parent of his children refused to allow him many of the visitation rights granted in the divorce decree. That was a problem, not a fact of life—something could be done about it. For what he felt were very valid reasons, however, he chose not to challenge her on it.

Unfortunately, his choice did not indicate to her his willingness to be reasonable and work with her. Rather, she saw it as a sign that she could push all she wanted and he would never respond. That initial "small" problem has now escalated into a veritable Pandora's box of abuses that can only be settled in court. When we accommodate problems, we almost always exacerbate them.

That is not to say that we must confront every situation head-on. Very often that is not the preferred way. It is critical, however, that we always make an informed decision. That means we understand why we respond in the manner we choose. A number of valid reasons exist for not attempting immediately to solve a problem. It may be that the problem is of such a minor nature that we genuinely do not believe that the desired results justify the effort. It may be that it is a very serious problem, but one for which confrontation will be an even more serious matter.

At that point, you and your spouse may need to engage in what is called "risk analysis management." In so doing, you ask the very serious question, "Does the potential damage done to my family by this problem justify the risk of damage which may be done if we take steps to correct it?" Such a question requires that we recognize the potential for damage both from the problem and from the solution.

As stepparent, you have a responsibility to be a steadying influence when the biological parent is faced with such a call. Many divorced parents feel that they must never give an inch and continually draw the line in the sand, almost seeking confrontation. At the slightest real or imagined affront, they seek redress in the courts, and the children are subject to the public enmity of their parents once again. In such a situation, the damage to the children more often comes from the solution than it does from the problem.

At the same time, however, many parents refuse to seek solutions to problems because to do so takes them out of their comfort zone. Meeting problems head-on is *not* easy. It takes moral fortitude, integrity, courage, and strength. It may also mean reliving old pains. And that is where you, as the new mate, the stepparent, can genuinely be a godsend.

One of the most intriguing passages in the teachings of Jesus is that passage that has come to be known as the Beatitudes. None of the beatitudes is more problematic for us than the second one: "Blessed are the meek." Meek? To be meek is to be blessed? No word has been done more damage by modern perceptions than has the word *meek*. In our minds, to be meek denotes a certain spinelessness, a cowardliness, the person afraid of his own shadow. Meekness certainly does not seem to be a characteristic to be cultivated.

Yet Jesus seemed quite sincere when he called on us to be meek. Surely he was not pronouncing a blessing on moral weakness. Perhaps the answer lies in looking at the manner in which the term was used in that day and time. Meekness was no reference to a lack of strength; rather, it carried a connotation of strength under control. In agrarian usage, it referred to the powerful animal whose strength had been harnessed and directed. It was not lack of strength, but control of strength.

Too often we use meekness as a panacea for weakness. When I was a fourth grader, I came home one day from school on the verge of tears because I had been bullied and threatened by an older and much larger sixth grader. No physical damage had been done because I had fled the scene so quickly. My father tried to comfort me by praising my biblical meekness, but meekness had nothing to do with it; I was terrified.

Just a few short days later, I watched as a sixth grade friend of mine walked away from a fight with the same bully. There was no terror in his eyes as he did so. He easily could have handled any physical threat, but he decided it simply was not worth the effort. He left not out of fear, but for the sake of prudence. For you see, he was meek.

So must it be in all those times we choose not to confront problems. It is so very easy to refuse to attempt to solve a problem because solutions can be costly. They may tear us from our comfort zone, exacting physical, emotional, spiritual, and relational costs. If, however, confrontation is what the situation demands, we must respond. When we recognize that God makes provision for his children, we can act boldly with assurance of provision. Then, whether we choose to confront or not to confront, we do so not from a position of weakness, but of meekness.

Not in the same way, but in the same spirit, we approach those situations which we call facts of life. We can only seek accommodation when we act from a spirit of meekness. The concept of meekness means that we recognize that God is ultimately in control and our only responsibility is to be faithful to his activity in our lives. Pridefulness stands in opposition to meekness. The prideful person will consistently attempt to change those things over which he has no control. In other words, he will treat a fact of life as a problem. You cannot solve reality; the terms cannot interact; you can only deal with it.

There are myriad reasons why we try to "solve reality." Many folks are just plain stubborn, and (in biblical language) take some sort of pleasure in kicking "against the goads." Others locked into a pattern of confrontation during the divorce proceedings ("Whatever he agrees to, I agree to the opposite.") and have never broken the habit. Still others may carry residual anger from the breakup of the family and will continually rail against factors over which they have no control. The bottom line, however, is that preoccupation with factors over which we have no control—be they court orders, manipulative actions on the part of an ex-spouse, financial limitations, or whatever—prevent the development of constructive responses within the family.

Taking Inventory

The constructive response begins with an inventory of the challenges that occupy your time. This inventory will take time, insight, and honesty. It is something that you and your spouse should do together. Begin the inventory with a detailed list of the challenges that shape your existence. Your list might include such factors as insufficient time with the children, an ex-spouse who manipulates the emotions of the children, residual anger from the divorce, and financial limitations.

These challenges are then divided into two categories: problems and realities. In the first category include those factors that you may address to resolve. In the second, include those areas over which you really have no control. As you attempt to make the determination, you should recognize that some of these factors will fall into both categories. For example, you may include in the inventory that your stepchild feels torn in her loyalty to her divorced parents. To some extent, this is a problem because you can help the child resolve the dissonance. On the other hand, some of the feelings may not be resolvable, and your response is to help her deal with the pressure she will always feel.

PROBLEMS   FACTS OF LIFE

Communication gaps

                    Manipulative ex-spouse

            Financial difficulty

Child's poor study habits

              Child's insecurity

                  Residual divorce guilt

                    Binding court decisions

                    Limited time w/children

Poor use of time together

Each family's chart will be different—even in regard to placement of identical items. For example, in a situation where there are excellent lines of communication with the ex-spouse, manipulation of the children might very well be an easily resolvable problem. At the same time, we all know that situations exist in which the biological parents of the child have no desire to work together for the well-being of the child. Thereby, in different families, we end up with varying charts.

Once your family's chart has been completed, you should establish a plan of action for dealing with those factors that you can do something about—the problems. The remainder of this book will offer some practical problem-solving approaches to some areas of difficulty common to many stepfamily relationships.

Acting Creatively—Making the Best of Life's Situations

We are still left with the very real difficulty of addressing those situations that are not going to change. In a church I once pastored, there was a divorced mother who had three high school-age children. The children's father used every contact with the children as an opportunity to belittle the mother and the family's Christian lifestyle. Her friends and family watched as she fought bitterness and constant anger toward her ex-husband. Disregarding the mother's pleas, the children's father was unwilling to end the behavior that was so destructive for the children. The breakthrough came when she reached the realization that she could never have any control over his actions—*but she could effectively deal with the reaction of the children.* At that point, she began to accept the fact of life—his attitude—and address the problem—how her children were responding to that criticism.

Problem solving is easy—that's a job any amateur parent can handle; dealing with the reality is the real challenge. But that is precisely what we must do if our families are to be all that God desires them to be. While the operative term for dealing with the problem is *resolution*, the key term for facts of life is *acceptance*. Acceptance does not mean that we like a situation; rather, it refers to the recognition that, from a human perspective, the situation is not going to change, and anger, bitterness, or malice which we direct toward the situation is counterproductive.

Acceptance then allows us to begin to seek *provision* within the situation. The concept of provision implies the meeting of needs from without. In other words, we depend upon divine intervention in unacceptable circumstances which we have been forced to accept. The story of Elijah serves as a case in point. After he had delivered the word from God that there would be no rain in Israel for a period of years, God sent him into the wilderness for his own protection. Elijah's circumstances in the barren wasteland certainly were not what he would most desire. For one matter, he had no food. God's provision to meet this need was that ravens would bring Elijah bread and meat each morning and evening. When Elijah accepted his life situation, God met Elijah's needs.

We should notice, however, that God's activity there almost certainly did not meet Elijah's desires. God used *ravens* to feed Elijah. Are you familiar with the eating habits of ravens? They are scavengers, picking up their food from the waste of others. The narrative of 1 Kings 17 does not suggest that what they brought him was any different from what they gathered for themselves. Elijah's wilderness sojourn was not a time of refreshment and relaxation; he ate carrion. But to seek from God our escape from what we may consider unacceptable circumstance misses the point. God's promise has always been provision in the midst of life's reality rather than escape from difficulty.

When we accept the unacceptable but unchangeable, we begin to form a partnership with God to make the best of whatever situation in which we find ourselves. Perhaps we can delineate three levels of responses that must be part and parcel of dealing with imposed reality. First, we practice *damage limitation.* That is, we attempt to minimize the negative effects of undesirable situations. With a problem, it is important to deal with the source of the problem rather than the symptom or effect. In dealing with a fact of life, however, the source is unalterable; therefore, it becomes imperative that the extent of damage caused by the undesirable situation is limited.

The example of the vindictive ex-spouse who constantly degraded his former wife in front of their children illustrates the point. The mother could not stop his diatribes. Therefore, her focus had to become the prevention of damage to the well-being of the children and their relationship with her. She accomplished the task in two ways. First, she acted in a consistent and loving manner toward the children, not indulging them, but demonstrating a constant concern for their well-being. Second, and perhaps most important, she refused to return evil for the evil done her. If she had engaged in the same type of behavior as the children's father, the children would have learned that such action was proper and fitting in dispute. Instead, they saw modeled the lifestyle of which Christ spoke. It should be added that she explained to the children that she was making a conscious and deliberate choice not to respond in kind. They needed to understand that their mother was not cowering in weakness (one of their father's charges), but that she was acting from a position of strength. As the children grew older, they began to see through their father's devices and learned well the lesson of returning good for evil.

Closely associated with damage limitation is the concept of *protection*. The only difference between the two is that damage limitation is reactive, while protection is proactive; that is, we act in anticipation of a situation rather than respond to one already existing. Of course, such activity means that we are not only conscientiously and consistently preparing our children to deal with any of life's contingencies, but also that we are paying close and careful attention to the often unrecognized clues of impending reality.

To achieve this kind of awareness demands that lines of communication between parent and child remain open and clear so that the parent can pick up small clues of what the child may be coming up against. At one time, it was quite common to speak of a "mother's intuition." This was not some paranormal perception, but the reception of minute communication by a mother who spent enough time with her children that she was quick to recognize when something was not quite "in tune."

Let me also suggest that the protection of the child is

also dependent upon close communication between the parents and our Heavenly Father. Such prayer not only allows God to impart his insight to us, but it is also itself an avenue of divine insulation for our children. Never underestimate the critical role that prayer plays in the protection of the family.

The Final Level: Seeing God Through It All

As we strive to limit damage and protect our children from pressures and temptations they should not have to face, at some point we recognize that there is only so much we can do. Then we are free to make the confession that their fate both temporally and ultimately does not lie in our hands, and we profess that God is in control. Binuclear families often live in greater awareness of God's graciousness and faithfulness than those not required to send their children to someone else's home at regular intervals. For, you see, these families genuinely understand that it is out of their hands, and in such recognition, true dependence upon divine intervention takes place. We do our best, but our children are in God's hands.

CHAPTER THREE

The Central Relationship

What God has joined together, let no man put asunder.
                    —Traditional Protestant
                    wedding blessing

It sure put us under, right or wrong.
                    —Country song

No doubt about it, marriage is tough. In the best of circumstances, marriages end up about an even bet for survival. In the United States, about half of all marriages end in divorce, a figure climbing so rapidly that it will be out of date by the time this book is published. Yet in spite of their past experiences, the vast majority of those who have experienced divorce will find a subsequent marriage waiting in the future.

If, in the best of circumstances, a marriage has just better than a 50 percent chance of being a lifelong relationship, what chance do second (or third, fourth, etc.) marriages have, for they are definitely not the best of circumstances? Clearly, few people learn from past mistakes; the failure rate for marriages in which one or both of the partners has experienced a previous divorce is markedly higher than for initial marriages. The average second marriage lasts six years. As a friend once remarked after a second divorce, "What I should have learned from my first marriage is that I'm no good at it."

The problem, it seems, is that people really *do not* learn from previous relationships. Instead, most divorced people waltz into subsequent marriage(s) in full and complete possession of all the quirks, faults, and immaturities that doomed the initial relationship. Toss in a stepchild or two, and the mixture that is a second marriage finds its potential for volatility greatly increased. A second marriage must face not only the stresses common to all marriages, but also the dynamics of extended relationships within the household, the baggage of the previous relationships, and perhaps even the subconscious acknowledgment that divorce has become a viable solution for a troubled marriage. It is little wonder that divorce statistics for subsequent marriages are so dismal.

"It won't happen again" must not be an idle avowal for the person entering a second marriage. Instead, it must be an affirmation of God's divine intent for any marriage and a recognition of the pitfalls therein—and of our confounding ability to step willingly into them. In those relationships in which one partner has experienced divorce and the other has not, such recognition may be even more necessary for the husband or wife entering marriage for the first time.

The Model and Priority

In many wedding ceremonies, the minister will note that the first institution ordained of God is the family. The first two chapters of Genesis comprise a superb recitation of relationships: between God and creation, between God and humankind, between humankind and the rest of creation. Notice, however, the capstone, the fulfillment of creation in these passages: not the speaking of the world into existence out of nothingness, not the bringing forth of living creatures after their kind, not even the creation of the first person. Although God looked upon the creation and pronounced it good, it was incomplete until the relationships were balanced. The story of creation is culminated only when Adam enters into a relationship with one of his own kind.

It is no coincidence that the ultimate stewardship presented to humankind—the creation of new life—can take place only within the context of relationship. From the beginning, God intended and designed that this ultimate gift which we share with him also be shared with another human being. Always in Scripture, the relationship between husband and wife is both pinnacle and foundation of all other relationships and institutions.

What was true in the beginning certainly stands today. Amidst a national debate on the importance of family values, both sides seem to overlook the most important concept in any such discussion: The integrity of the primary relationship immediately and directly affects all secondary and tertiary relationships and institutions. The man who lies to his wife should not be trusted in corporate relationships. A woman who abuses her position in the home may be expected to be abusive in other

37

relationships. I am constantly amazed at the stream of ministers who have been repeatedly unfaithful to the institution of marriage and yet are welcomed back to their pulpits by open-armed congregations who never recognize that the lack of fidelity may be a character trait that infects secondary relationships. Throughout Scripture, fidelity to the institution of marriage is portrayed as a bellwether for all other relationships. If the husband/wife relationship is not healthy, none of the consequent relationships can be well-founded.

The primacy of this relationship is an especially valid concept for the stepfamily. The natural inclination in the stepfamily is to focus first on the children. Such an inclination is an outgrowth of the God-given affection and care which is fostered in our lives to perpetuate divine intent for our families. Like any other of God's gifts, however, this focus becomes abusive when it is not kept in its proper perspective. "She lives for her children" may be intended as a compliment to a mother, but it may also be an indictment of the health of the primary relationship between husband and wife.

In the stepfamily, it is very easy for the relationship between natural parent and child to take precedence over the relationship between wife and husband. Many of the reasons for such a situation reflect valid concerns: the parent may rightly view a daughter or son as the innocent victim of divorce and attempt to compensate with extra protection and attention; the parent/child relationship was established before the new husband/wife relationship and is, therefore, the first loyalty; the focus of our society is on children, and the home reflects that priority.

Regardless of the valid concerns expressed by making the parent/child relationship the most important one in the family, the damage done to the family is the same. If the primary relationship between wife and husband is not sound—not placed in the first position—neither can the relationship between parent and child fulfill its divinely commissioned task. If you sacrifice the health of your marriage for what you perceive to be the well-being of your children, you will almost certainly lose both.

The most important teaching function in the family consists of modeling lifestyles and values. By definition, stepchildren have already seen one family model how *not* to do relationships. Reinforce that imaging of failure in a second marriage, and the children will have a prescription for the failure of their own future marriage. If a parent genuinely loves a child or stepchild, the marriage relationship must provide a strong and secure foundation for teaching the child the manner in which God intends us to form relationships of love with one another. Genuine concern for the child demands that the husband/wife relationship must be the priority. After all, the worst thing that can happen to the child is that he or she becomes the innocent victim of a second divorce.

But They Were Here First

Observing a situation of potentially volatile friction between a stepmother and stepdaughter, a friend remarked, "She'd [the stepmother] better realize his daughter was here first, and if push comes to shove, his ultimate loyalty lies with his daughter." The friend was right, of course, but how tragic that the stepmother and father had let such a situation evolve. The fact of the matter is, however, that the natural affection, loyalty, and bond between parent and child must be nurtured, while, at the same time, placed in a noncompetitive position toward the newly formed husband/wife relationship.

The biological parent's recognition of the natural and proper loyalty to the child is the first step in making sure that the relationship maintains its necessary position in the family. Such a recognition allows the natural parent at least a measure of perspective. We have all known fathers and mothers who, while claiming abject objectivity, always took their children's side in any conflict, without regard to fault. They made the easy mistake of confusing support for their children with blind loyalty. We also have seen a father or a mother who consistently chose to join with the children in an "us against you" relationship with the other parent. Such situations occur because parents' loyalty and protectiveness toward their children as God-given gifts are as subject to human abuse as any other divine provision. In the stepfamily—a life-situation in which the divisions in relationships become even more strained—the natural parent must recognize this loyalty as a critical commodity, but one that must always be kept in proper perspective with the other relationships within the home.

It is equally important that the stepparent recognize this loyalty—and respond to it properly. Because parental concern for a child is a natural reflection of God's love for us, the stepparent should promote that relationship, not compete with it—even if the child wishes, consciously or unconsciously, to foster that competition. When a newborn enters a family, older siblings are often jealous of the attention the newborn receives. Think how much more difficult it must be for the child to see the birth of a new adult relationship.

When you became a focus of love for your spouse, you may have resolved many problems for your new husband or wife, but you brought a whole new set of relational problems for your stepchildren—*problems that are not mitigated by the child's love for you or enjoyment of your company.* First, you destroyed any dreams that the child might have held for Mom and Dad to get back together (and, surprisingly, children brought from even the worst home situations seem to almost always harbor such hopes).

Second, older children have often assumed parental protection roles toward their divorced parents. They don't want to see Mom or Dad hurt again and are deeply suspicious that this is precisely what lies in store in the new relationship. Third, despite our best reassurances, few children can comprehend that love is not a finite package that can be divided only in so many ways. They are convinced that love for you means less affection for them. Whatever the difficulty, the new stepparent is the source of the problem and, thereby, the child may focus extreme jealousy at the marriage relationship.

How may we then respond? We begin by affirming all of the love relationships in the family. It is important that the stepparent find time alone with the stepchild and express support for those relationships. The stepchild must be made to understand that his or her family has been enlarged and consequently enriched, and that the enrichment is not a threat to the relationship between biological parent and child. After all, the child probably did not have a choice in bringing a new adult into the family. Your affirmation of the already existing relationship between parent and child and demonstration that you make that relationship even better can make the child feel that she would have made the same choice if she were the one doing the choosing.

My wife and I have a simple and unnegotiable rule in our home: When we have occasional differences which are settled in front of the children, neither of us has the prerogative of an emotional blowup. The reasons for such an agreement are myriad, but, as much as anything else, we do not want our daughters to have the option of choosing sides. In such a situation, no matter which parent is chosen as in the right (and it will almost always be the biological parent), all sides lose. A fracture in the family benefits no one. While wife and husband may quickly resolve the central issue, the residual fallout may remain with the child throughout the relationship.

Equally important, the stepparent must guard against feelings of jealousy toward the child. Those entering a marriage relationship should be sufficiently mature and confident in their spouse's love so that they feel no threat from their spouse's son or daughter. Unfortunately, that is often not the case. The situation becomes infinitely more complicated if both partners bring children into the relationship. It often becomes a "mine versus yours" situation. In the dynamics of a new family, we must take great care never to force the parent into a "them or me" situation. Never require a parent to choose between a child which God has given them and a spouse which they have chosen. Even if you win, everybody loses.

The bottom line is pretty clear: Unless both adults commit fully to making the marriage a success, failure looms on the near horizon. That is not just failure for the marriage, but failure for the children also, who will have missed an opportunity to learn what a husband/wife relationship can be. If, however, the couple dedicates themselves to working through the difficult times together, then the children can catch a glimpse of genuine marriage. In such a joint commitment, the essence of marriage is revealed: The fact that one person cannot make the commitment alone, cannot make the marriage environment what it should be, reveals to the family and to the world God's plan for shared responsibility.

Not a Model Marriage, but a Marriage That Models

It is little wonder that statistics reveal that children of divorce run a much higher risk of divorce in their own marriages than those who grew up in a stable, one-marriage family. Educators inform us that children learn most from what is modeled in front of them. The old adage "Do as I say, not as I do" simply does not work. If children see that the bailout of divorce is a viable solution to the problems encountered in any marriage, the lesson will be imprinted upon them far better than any instruction stressing the sanctity of marriage can ever be.

Even more tragic may be the damage done to the child's image of God and of the church. When I was a college student, I helped lead day camps for inner-city children. The instruction received in an orientation session impressed upon me how vital a sound family environment really is for our concept of God. We were told to be very careful about using the term "Father" for God and the term "family" for the Christian community.

For many of those children, "father" was someone who was either not a part of their lives or someone who was a source of continual abuse. "Family" was not a place of protection, joy, and sharing, but only an environment to be escaped. How tragic! The best chance we have to teach children about God has been taken from us. It is not just a problem for inner-city families; it is a problem that crosses all economic, social, racial, and religious lines.

The stepfamily, therefore, has the opportunity to be a part of the solution rather than the problem. Children of divorce have already seen the model fail once. The stepfamily is then divinely given the opportunity to be an agent of redemption—and no higher privilege is given by God. This opportunity begins with a vision and a commitment. The vision is of what a family can be and of what it can accomplish in the lives of the parents and the children. The family can be a place where we learn about God's care for us, a place where we experience unconditional love, a place where we come to understand absolute commitment. The commitment is a determination to expend the effort necessary to see the vision become a reality.

The family provides the moral, spiritual, social, and psychological foundation for its members only when both parents are committed to the priority of the marriage. The children and the world will learn only what they see. A lesson in kind comes from the charitable organization Habitat for Humanity, which provides inexpensive housing for families in economic distress. A sign outside a Habitat construction project reads, "This house is a sermon about God's love." The message of the sign is clear: People understand only what they experience. A low-income family can grasp what God's love for them means when they see Christians providing them a place to live. In like manner, your stepchildren can understand commitment and the sanctity of the marriage relationship only when they see the presence of the love and faithfulness which are the hallmark of the Christian home.

CHAPTER
FOUR

A Walk
in Small Shoes

To each a looking glass reflects the other
that doth pass.
>   —Charles Horton Cooley

It is often a matter of perspective and position.
The new marriage that you approached with eager expectation and perhaps a touch of trepidation may have
brought quite different emotions for your stepchildren.
In fact, when faced with a subsequent marriage, most
children find themselves in the middle of a balancing act
of competing feelings. They feel the nervous excitement
of the upcoming ceremony, the final realization that
Mom and Dad are not going to get together again, the
joy of seeing a parent really in love, jealousy at that same
love, budding affection for the new stepparent, and
perhaps fear of the dynamics between their two families.
That is a lot for a child to balance. Add to the mixture a
few adolescent hormones, and it can become too much
to handle.

The management of new relationships, whether in

marriage or otherwise, commands a significant alloca-
tion of emotional, mental, and physical energies. In
today's high-pressure world, many corporations periodically require stress indexing for all executives. In such
stress tests, the majority of indicators deal with changes
in relationships: marriage, divorce, death of a family
member, change in employment. The greater the number of these factors in an individual's life within a given
time span, the higher the stress level. The medical
community offers the unanimous opinion that, if an
individual attempts to integrate too many stress factors
in a short period of time, the body will rebel. Therefore,
these stress tests are remarkably accurate forecasters of
major health problems. God simply did not design us,
emotionally or physically, to be overloaded with pressure.

Psychologists tell us that children, too, face stress at
historically unprecedented levels. The schools they at-
tend are not the schools of twenty or thirty years ago.
They know pressures that did not exist when we were
children. When my older stepdaughter was a third
grader, she walked up to me with the question "What is
AIDS?" I responded that we would sit down and discuss
her question when we both had more time. She then
responded, "That's okay. We are going to hear a report
about it in school tomorrow." We made time to talk,
right then.

Life for our children may not be cookies and milk
after school, summers at Granddad's farm, and wide-
eyed innocence and wonder at creation around them.
They live in a confusing and demanding—and sometimes demeaning—world. Therefore, as never before,

home must be a refuge, a place where the confusion and pressure go away. Especially in the stephome, our children must feel the warmth of God and the security of familial acceptance and love. And you can make it such a place.

So Many Changes

Suspend your adult perspective for a few minutes, and live in the world of your children. Look at the pressures brought to bear upon them which are specifically related to your family status. On the short term, as we discussed in Chapter 1, the children face the demands of emotional immediacy in a manner traditional families never experience. I cannot remember a time before I loved my parents. I do not remember learning house rules. I never "met" my parents (nor my brother or sister, since I was the youngest child). All these relationships were a part of my life from day one, and I grew into them as I matured.

The stepchild never has the opportunity to assimilate relationships and to be assimilated by them. Instead, the relationship springs into the stepchild's life in full bloom. Constance Green records the conversation of two young boys in *I and Sproggy* (Dell, 1981):

> "It's easy for you to say," Adam told him. "How'd you like it? A total stranger practically related to you and everything coming into your house and you have to be polite and act like everything's peachy when it isn't? That's not the easiest thing in the world, Charlie. Put yourself in my shoes. It's darn tough."

It is darn tough. When we expect our children immediately to respect, honor, and love an adult—whom they may have very good reasons to resent—we are asking a lot of them. And that is just one factor that the new stepchild has to face.

The stepchildren are also called upon to assimilate new rules, as well as new authority figures. For many house rules, there is no "real" right or wrong. Rather, each home has its own set of standards and its own "right" way of doing things. When Susan and I married, her house rules were not my house rules; her way of doing things was not my way of doing things. Some of our procedural differences were rather inconsequential (we still cannot agree on the best way to make a bed), some more substantive. In most newly established homes, some common ground is established. A working compromise is found in which the husband brings some rules, the wife brings some rules, and some are generated by the relationship. The important focus in the establishment of the relationship, however, is the partnership in developing these rules. Husband and wife share the task of establishing the standards for the home.

For the child, things are quite different. First of all, the child is rarely involved in the negotiation of new house rules. The parents begin to find their common ground. They find the areas in which they are willing to compromise, the areas in which they are not willing to compromise, and they evolve the new home system— largely without input from the children. Thereby, the child is not only called upon to deal with a new person in his or her life, but also suddenly discovers that the way they have *always* done things may not be good enough anymore. The child immediately realizes who is to blame for the imposition of new rules and new standards: the stepparent. If the family is not careful, the child may begin to associate any new rule, standard of behavior, or responsibility as an imposition from the stepparent, even if the change has more to do with the child's increasing age and ability to meet obligations than it does with the change in the nature of the household.

. If the child is also required to follow the discipline and instruction of the new stepparent, another factor has been introduced into an already confusing equation. It very well may be that the new stepparent should be involved in the discipline of the children. (We will discuss that question in detail in Chapter 6.) But when the stepparent disciplines, we must recognize that an additional level of conflict in the home has been added.

Whose Child Am I?

If emotional immediacy and questions of discipline are factors in short-term stress for the child, family loyalty and identity, while not affecting the child as acutely, are chronic sources of emotional wrestling for the child. A stepmother tells of the first weekends when her two elementary age stepdaughters would come for their visitation time. The little girls would play and love and visit with their father with all the affection and joy that two little girls can muster.

When the stepmother came around, however, the older girl immediately changed. She became haughty, rude, angry. She called her stepmother inappropriate names; she refused to obey her stepmother. Any approach—be it one of love, be it one of discipline, be it one of simple conversation—would send the girl flying into a rage. After a period of time, the younger sister came to talk to her stepmother concerning the older. She professed confusion, explaining that their older sister had told her that if she was nice to her stepmother, it meant "she really didn't love Mommy anymore." Is it any wonder that the older child refused to enter into a relationship with her stepmother?

Sadly, her father and stepmother discovered that the source of the little girl's perception was the mother of the girls. She had explained to the girls that they were not to be touched, to be hugged, to have any type of relationship with their stepmother because she was a mean person. Fortunately, through years of consistent love, constant returning of good for evil, and general pleasantness, both little girls have discovered that their stepmother is a fine Christian woman who wants the very best for them.

While most cases may not be that extreme nor may most parents abuse their children psychologically as in this situation, questions of loyalty occur in almost every stepfamily relationship where both natural parents are still involved in the lives of the children. In most cases, the child will never recognize the dynamic and label it as a question of loyalty. But it will be there, and the watchful eye of a loving family will recognize it for what it is.

The stepchild is also called upon to develop a composite identity: "Am I who I am because I am a part of my mother and stepfather's family, or do I find my identity in my father and stepmother's family, or am I some weird combination of both?" Our understanding of who we are is intrinsically and inseparably linked to our familial history. As we read Scripture, we cannot help noting how important a sense of heritage, of community, of birthright is to those who peopled the stories. The pride of the Israelite was his ability to trace his lineage back to Abraham, to know that his family came from one location. The whole story of the Exodus is a story of returning to roots, to a sense of identity. It is a story of knowing who they were by knowing from whence they had come.

From the time I was ten years old until I was an adult, I grew up in a small farming and ranching community. My identity is inextricably linked to that community and my family's position in the community. I remember well the first time I took my wife back to the region where I grew to manhood. I showed her the mountains I climbed, the desert paths I loved to walk, the high school I attended, the drive-in where my friends gathered during teenage years. All these were—are—a part of my identity.

A much deeper part of my identity, however, came from my relationship with my family. I learned very early that there were certain things that Nowells did or did not do. Certain standards of behavior were expected because that was who we were. In my childhood, less appeal for good behavior was made to right and wrong than to "remember who you are."

In 1902, with the aphorism "To each a looking glass reflects the other that doth pass," psychologist Charles Horton Cooley introduced the world to the concept of the looking-glass self. To wit, we gain our understanding of who we are by the reflection of ourselves that we see in those around us. In other words, self-identity comes from the understanding of who we are that is gained in relationship with those around us. When friends and family react to a certain behavior negatively, the child learns that some behavior is not acceptable. He learns that other behavior is perfectly acceptable when others react positively toward it. He learns that he is a good person when those around him treat him with love, as someone of value. He learns that he is an unworthy person when those around him do not have time for him.

What reflection of themselves do stepchildren see in the lives of their families? If it is a consistently positive reflection, the stepchild will gain a consistent sense of identity. If, instead, that reflection changes every other weekend, the stepchild might not be quite sure who she is. If during the week the child is rewarded for good behavior, discovers that conversation about God and Christian values is just a part of her life, learns that we return good for evil, she will develop a self-concept consistent with such values. If the child has one family that supports such values and one that belittles these values ("We don't do things that way"), then the child may have an identity crisis on her hands. "Who am I? Who is my family? What do we believe?"

Over the last twenty years, a number of studies have consistently demonstrated that children to a remarkable degree reflect the values and interests of their parents. The mirroring is so consistent that, for seven of the last eight presidential elections, the *Weekly Reader* classroom poll has predicted the winner. The kids vote the way their parents are going to vote. Thus, when children find two value systems, two systems of identity, they are forced to make a choice, not of which system they most appreciate or which one is most logically suited for their lifestyles, but of who they are. That is a choice no child is prepared to make. If the child is forced to make such decisions, the choice will give rise to a host of identity problems for the child.

Misdirected Anger

In his novel *Love Song*, Father Andrew M. Greeley crafts the story of a young Chicago assistant district attorney driven by a destructive quest for paternal approval. In her zeal, she turns her prosecutorial guns upon a successful Chicago businessman and philanthropist, who, ironically, is the one man who genuinely loves her for who she is. Ultimately, this love overwhelms the family dynamics that have blinded her to her own motives. It is in the midst of her struggle to measure up to her father that she discovers that he is an unremarkable individual, not the superman that she imagined him to be, deserving neither idolatry nor scorn; he is simply a father with all the frailties and foibles that characterize each of us. She makes this realization, however, only in the face of the unconditional love, acceptance, and forgiveness given her by the man she had dedicated her life to destroying.

In such a story lies a certain parable for the stepfamily. When a divorce occurs in a family with children, it is never merely an act between husband and wife. Instead, it is an act *between* husband and wife and an act *against* the children. No matter to what length parents go to explain that the divorce is not the children's fault and that they are not being deserted, the children still feel a sense of responsibility for the breakup. They also perceive that a great wrong is being done them.

The greatest anger is usually directed at the non-resident parent, which, in most cases, is the father. While most children will at some point ask the mother, "Why did you make Daddy leave?" the much more persistent question is directed toward the father: "Why did you leave us?" The child has no choice but to accept the father's answer no matter how inadequate it may be—and it is always inadequate. In such a dynamic reside the roots of budding anger, an anger that must be addressed in the stepfamily.

In the stepfamily, the child may initiate a defense mechanism which psychologists call displacement of feeling. Displacement is the process by which an individual subconsciously transfers feelings (anger) from an inappropriate object (the absent parent) to a more appropriate object (the stepparent). Thus, the child, who on the surface is openly hostile toward the stepparent, may actually be living out feelings of anger toward a parent. The complexity of the dynamics of this displacement may be compounded by the fact that the child honestly does not recognize that the real anger is toward the parent. He may think that he really is angry with a new stepfather, even if he is unable to articulate any reason for the anger.

It is quite easy to see how displacement occurs. A child in a family with a non-resident parent may feel a need to be an apologist for that parent. Paradoxically, though the child may himself be critical of the absent parent, the child must believe that the parent is a good person and that the parent genuinely cares about the child. (Remember the discussion concerning identity and self-worth?) Therefore, the child believes that the parent cannot have stopped loving him. If the parent had left the child, it would be a devastating blow to the child's self-worth. Therefore, the child cannot maintain an anger toward the non-resident parent, for to do so would suggest that the parent had done something wrong toward the child. So a new object for the brewing anger must be found—and the stepparent is the most convenient target.

The transference of anger is often accompanied by an idealization of the absent parent. Some children very conveniently forget the bad—the arguments, the shouting, possible abuse, emotional neglect. Instead, everything was great before Dad left. The child takes whatever good moments can be recalled and makes them the norm for "the way things used to be." A little boy speaks of days at the ballpark: "Dad always took me to the game, never missed one." A conversation with the mother, however, might reveal that once or twice a year the son was allowed to accompany Dad to the baseball stadium when one of his buddies had an extra ticket. It had never been a regular thing, but in the child's mind it became the idealized standard.

In the nuclear home, idealization serves a necessary and healthy function. In the development of the child, a love which dotes provides a very necessary ingredient for the family. Parents love the child unconditionally, which helps the child develop self-pride, confidence, and esteem, which are foundational for mental health.

In the same manner, young children have a very specialized picture of their parents. The parents' word is accepted without question; the parents' values are seen as normative. Anyone disagreeing with the child's parents is simply wrong. As the child matures and becomes more sophisticated in thought and judgment, the child learns to love, honor, and respect without the same level of idealization. In the nuclear family, an unconditional love allows the family to become a haven of protection, a nest to which the child can return as she learns to stretch her wings and grow.

The stepfamily, conversely, provides no biological impetus for doting or idealization. Most stepparents are well aware of their stepchildren's faults. Most stepchildren see every flaw in the stepparent's personality. Therefore, the stepparent is often left to compete with an idealized non-resident parent. The problem is exacerbated when the stepparent is the one who has to be there through the ins and outs and difficulties of everyday life, while the idealized absent parent sees the child only on weekend visits which may be little more than regularly scheduled play days for the child.

If the stepparent falls into the trap of competition with the idealized parent, he will always lose. The stepparent loses even if he or she does a much better job of parenting than the absent parent could or can ever do. It is not a contest judged on performance, but a contest judged by perceptions that may have no basis in reality. Therefore, it is imperative that the stepparent offer creative responses to the dynamics that compose the stepfamily relationship.

There Are No Ex-parents

Dr. Lyle Joyce of Minneapolis, Minnesota, is one of

the world's foremost experts on heart transplants and artificial heart devices. His greatest difficulty in transplant situations is organ rejection. The body's immune system recognizes when that which is foreign is imposed upon it—even when the imposition is for the body's own good. It will fight to reject the alien object, even at the cost of its own life. Transplant surgeons are thereby forced to give huge doses of anti-autoimmune drugs to suppress the body's own defenses. Even so, very often the body cannot be made to accept that which it does not recognize as its own.

The same is true in the stepfamily. Under any circumstance, the stepfamily is not the natural biological situation. All children naturally react negatively to the stepfamily, at least to some degree. This negativity may be initially overwhelmed by the excitement of "I have a new daddy!" (especially in younger children), or it may be repressed and unseen for years, but it is almost always there.

Thus, it is critical that the stepparent and the custodial parent recognize that the home they provide for their children is not the same home that is provided when both biological parents are present. If both biological parents are alive, and often even if one is not, both the parent and the non-resident parent will have tremendous influence on the development of the child. There may be ex-husbands, ex-lovers, and ex-friends, but there are no ex-parents. Parents may be dead, may be absent, may be uninvolved, but they are nonetheless parents.

If you are a stepparent, you must recognize that you can never replace the parent of the child—but that fact in no way lessens your importance nor your responsibility for the child. Instead, it demands that you constructively act to make the stephome meet all the needs common to every child as well as those needs peculiar to the stepchild.

When stepparents begin to consider themselves the "real" parent, they attempt to usurp a necessary role in the child's life. At the moment that attempt occurs, the stepparent has placed himself—and the child—in a very dangerous and volatile situation. Instead, the stepparent must recognize the stepfamily for what it is and attempt to make it the very best that it can be. Such recognition is not a denigration of the importance or vitalness of the stepfamily. Rather, it affirms that the stepparent, as part of the stepfamily, can be used of God to provide essential nurture, support, love, and stability which may have been taken away by the breakup of the stepchild's family. This can be done without ever attempting to replace the natural parent.

Losing by Trying Too Hard

Western literature is replete with stories of the evil stepparent. From *Cinderella* to *The Stepfather,* we are bombarded with tales of stepparents of evil intent, selfish motives, and even criminal designs. The stepparent, often depicted as a monster of abuse and neglect, gets a lot of bad press. The reality is most certainly much different. The stepparent may be the one who is always there for the child, a special friend and advocate in a tough world. The problem is usually not neglect nor abuse of power, rather—especially in the Christian home—the problem is that we try too hard to be everything to our stepchildren.

When the stepparent enters into the new family relationship, he or she usually feels that "the kids are part of the deal." The good, conscientious Christian stepparent will often try to move right into the mix that is the reconstituted family and try not to be a stepparent, or even just a parent, but a superparent. Because they *do* recognize that they will be compared to the absent parent, the stepmother or stepfather will become a "most" parent: the most exciting, the most understanding, the most caring, the most fun, the most glamorous.

The stepchild may initially be awed by such a display, but the act will grow old very quickly. Stepchildren do not feel the obligation to accept immediately this new person into their lives. Instead, they need room to grow into the relationship. As a result, the stepparent and stepchild find their relationship discordant, out of tune with each other. Initially, the stepparent tries to establish the close bond, only to be rejected. The stepparent then pulls back, placing distance in the relationship. As the child grows more comfortable with the new family situation, he tries to build the bridge toward the stepparent who has already structured distance between them. Both stepchild and stepparent can be hurt and confused by the process.

Giving Love Time

Let's not paint the picture too bleak. In the scenario we have just discussed, the most important factor is that both the stepchild and the stepparent genuinely do want a good relationship. In the vast majority of stepfamilies—especially those with younger stepchildren—both the adults and the children want the relationships within the family to be strong, loving, and nurturing. The problem lies in the dynamics; it is a question of "How do we get there from here?"

We may find our answer when we reformulate the question. Perhaps what we should ask is "*When* do we get there from here?" It really is a question of time. We must learn to allow time for the relationship to grow—after all, even biological parents get nine months to get used to the idea of someone new in the family. Don't push; don't be a superparent; don't feign love that is not yet present.

It is fascinating to listen to stepparents recount the stories of when they first realized that they really did love their stepchildren. More often than not, the affirmation of love occurred as the stepparent anguished over some problem the stepchild was facing. The stepparent discovered genuine care and concern for the well-being of the child.

So often for the Christian stepparent, the reality of love becomes a part of our lives as we spend time in prayer for the child. Do you really want to grow a deeper love for your stepchildren? Pray for them. If your stepchildren are small, kneel beside their bed after they are asleep and seek God's protection for them. If they are older, spend time in prayer with them. In such moments, genuine, lasting love comes to life.

The moral of all this? Love can come and usually does come, but it must be given room and time to grow. It cannot be manufactured or forced but must be given birth in the relationship.

The Critical Question

In the Christian classic *In His Steps,* Charles M. Sheldon tells the story of a town in which the question "What would Jesus do?" becomes the prerequisite for any action. The community is transformed as the townspeople reorient their lives to make them responsive to that question. In like manner, many of the conflicts within the stepfamily, and even between the two families that are part of the stepchild's life, could be resolved if we would allow one question to form the context for our activity: "Is what I am doing in the best interest of the child?"

Unfortunately, parents and stepparents alike more often invoke "the interest of the child" to justify actions that have nothing to do with the child's well-being and everything to do with self-gratification. One of the most common but harmful occurrences in the life of the child with divorced parents is the verbal attack (the "putting down") of one parent by the other parent or by a nonresident stepparent. Many families have recognized that consistent degradation of one parent to the children by the other is simply a fact of life. What is most amazing, however, is that, in most such cases, the parent launching the attack will claim it is for the good of the children.

One perceptive third grader gave her perspective of such a situation. "When Dad complains about what a terrible mother you are, and always says bad things about you, it's like he's shooting bullets at you. What Dad doesn't see is that the bullets have to go through us before they can hit you because we're the ones that have to hear him. You don't get hurt; we do." Is that really doing the children any good?

CHAPTER FIVE

Facing the World

Children stand more in need of example than criticism.

—Joseph Joubert

It was the first day of a new adventure for my wife and me: we were volunteering as computer instructors at our daughters' school. Many of the children already knew us, and we anticipated a good working relationship with all of them. We felt that we were prepared for almost any classroom situation. We were not, however, prepared for the dynamics imposed by our particular family situation. Shortly after the first session began, I overheard one of my stepdaughter's friends whisper, "Jinnifer, why do you call your dad 'David'?"

With only a slight hint of a cloud crossing her eyes, Jinnifer replied, "Because he is my stepdad, not my real dad." Oh. This friend was not the only one of my stepdaughter's classmates and friends not to have the relationship quite figured out. Only about half of these children refer to me as Dr. Nowell; many just assume Susan and I have the same last name as the girls.

We have all heard the expression, "If it looks like a duck, walks like a duck, and sounds like a duck, it is probably safe to call it a duck." Not so with the stepfamily. Since the stepfamily is visually no different from the biological family, the assumption of anyone meeting a man and woman with children is that they are encountering a traditional family. The awkward situations that are part of the stepfamily's life arise out of that mistaken identity. In the very same context, however, is born the golden opportunity to model for our children genuine graciousness and the ability to rise above difficult circumstances.

In the public arena we are often left to explain our different last names and different relationships both to close friends and, occasionally, to complete strangers. What must be kept in mind, however, is that these transitional situations—the settings in which friends and new acquaintances learn how to approach our families—are as difficult for those we encounter as they are for us. Indeed, these situations are as difficult as we as parents allow them to be.

When the stepfamily meets the public, the stepfamily must take control of the situation. Those who are met by the stepfamily will consistently look for clues to the best way to address the stepfamily, the relationship between the members of the stepfamily, the level of comfort in the interaction between the children's two families, and, finally, the general comfort that the stepfamily has with their life situation. If the stepparent and the present parent are defensive, quick to anger, or demonstrate discomfort and awkwardness, friends and family will quickly pick up on those cues and reflect them in their interaction with the stepfamily. Therefore, early on in the relationship, the whole stepfamily needs to become comfortable with the public aspect of their lives.

No less than the parent and the stepparent, the children of the stepfamily must also learn to deal with the difficult situation. Children do not like to be "different"; peer pressure to conform is pronounced on children of any age. For younger children, however, this pressure is especially evident when questions of the viability and legitimacy of the child's family situation arise. Though almost half of all American children live in nontraditional families, the stepchild often feels that he or she is the only one with more than one set of parents. As a child whose parents had divorced and married new mates said to me, "No one understands what it is like. I just wish I could have one family like everyone else."

The family must do two things to help children deal with meeting the public. First, the family must be open and honest in talking about the realities of their lives together. Questions about the difficulty of meeting the public, recognition of challenges inherent in the stepfamily, and acknowledgment of the sometimes difficult dynamics of relationships between the children's two families must be openly and honestly addressed. By so doing, the reconstituted family provides the children with the tools to address the emotional challenges they will face throughout their lives.

Second, but no less important, the present parent and the stepparent must help the children to understand that *awkward* does not mean *bad.* Too often, we allow ourselves to develop a sense of dread for any situation with which we feel uncomfortable. As we do, we begin to see those situations as not just socially awkward, but as objectively "wrong" or "bad." At that point, we have traded a comfort level realization for a moral judgment and have greatly raised our level of resistance to the situation. Successful persons are those who can recognize situations for what they are and deal with them accordingly, unlike those who elevate every context into a morality play or a crisis situation.

Throughout a child's life, he or she will face uncomfortable situations related to family, job, and social settings. If the child can learn at an early age to operate within the context of these difficulties with grace and a sense of class, the child will have mastered a valuable life lesson. As a stepparent, one of the greatest gifts you can give your children is the ability to rise above circumstance and to act with courage, aplomb, and control in any situation.

Renewing Old Acquaintances

More lies are told at class reunions than in any other setting—with good reason. Not many of us want those who knew us well to think that we are less than the epitome of the success story. Therefore, when time for the old homecoming rolls around, we make sure that we wear our best suit or most flattering dress, that our skin glows with a fresh tan, and that our car is polished to the hilt. Unfortunately, at many reunions, we do more than just put our best foot forward. The class reunion is often the time when stories about our jobs are enhanced, our children are made out to be just a little bit more successful than they really are, and our financial worth is considerably inflated. We want our long-ago friends to know just how far we have come.

In much the same way, remarried couples often "perform" for acquaintances known in the antecedent marriage. One of the most difficult aspects of divorce is the fear of judgment from friends and family. We rarely so much fear a judgment of sin (though sometimes we do), as we do a judgment of failure. We all want to be successful. When a marriage falls apart, the indictment is not pronounced on what we have done, but upon who we are; the judgment is that something is wrong with us that prevented us from succeeding at one of life's most important tasks.

Therefore, when the divorced individual remarries, the tendency is to show the world "See, I really can be successful." To accomplish such a task, the remarried individual will often inflate the positive character traits of the new spouse to a degree beyond realistic levels. The new spouse becomes the ultimate husband, the super father, the ideal friend—often in direct contrast to the ex-spouse.

Old friends are not easily fooled. They recognize the game for what it is, and the naturalness and the ease of transition to acceptance of the new mate becomes impaired. As the spouse of a divorced person you must realize that your spouse's friends possibly knew him or her only in the context of the previous relationship. Therefore, these friends have to establish an acquaintanceship—not to mention a relationship—with you as husband or wife of your spouse.

In many cases, your spouse's friends may have maintained a relationship with the previous marriage partner. If you are brought in as the ideal mate, in constant contrast to the ex-spouse, loyalty to the ex-spouse who is still their friend may demand a certain distance in the newly formed relationship with you. If you compete with their longtime friend, you will always lose, and the difficulty of the transition will be immeasurably exacerbated.

An additional factor can be added to the mixture. Many of these friends and family members who have long-established relationships with your spouse's family knew your stepchildren long before you did. They have memories of events and personality traits which you never knew. In a very real sense, they can claim a "squatter's right" to your stepchildren, a right that they may feel antedates, and therefore supersedes, your relationship. They were here first. It may be very difficult for them to see you correcting the children. It may be difficult for them to see the emerging affection between you and your stepchildren. If they have maintained a relationship with the children's other parent, you may appear to be the interference; you may appear to be the source of friction.

One stepfather tells the story of his first visit to his new in-laws' home after the wedding. While his wife was outside, his stepson caused a problem that demanded immediate attention. In the middle of the stepfather's reprimand to the young boy, the child's grandmother interjected herself into the situation with an "I'll handle this." After the scenario repeated itself several times, the family realized that the grandmother was simply unwilling to allow the perceived interloper to discipline her grandchild. The mother and stepfather were forced to confront a very difficult situation.

Sometimes it seems that it would be easier to cut all the strings and start over, to pack up our families and our homes, lock, stock, and barrel, and move to a place where no one knows us. We could find a new job, develop new friends. That might be the easiest way, but in most cases, it is almost certainly not the best way.

Your stepchildren have already experienced at least one brutal interruption of their lives. When their parents divorced, it probably seemed to them that the very stability that assured their present and their future had been torn from under them. The constancy of maintained relationships with family and friends allows them to gain a sense of consistency and steadiness in an unsure world. So the children, as well as your spouse, need to see that these relationships can be maintained and prosper even in a new environment.

When Four Parents Are Present

German theologian Paul Tillich suggests that only two types of sin beset humankind, each a result of refusing to be what God has designed us to be. The first type occurs when we are unwilling to live up to divine intentions for us. We debase ourselves by acting more like animals than like the crown of creation. When we behave promiscuously, when we are driven by animal passions, when we let rage govern our actions, we fall into this category of sin. The other type of sin occurs as we refuse to acknowledge God as God and usurp his prerogatives for ourselves. The sins of self-centeredness, judgmentalism, and pride are the hallmark of such trespass.

Perhaps no other venue offers the opportunity for greater demonstration of both types of offense than does the public interaction when four parents of one set of children are present. At the very time when it seems that parents should be on their best behavior, demonstrating graciousness in front of family and friends, we instead often find parents who seem intent upon demonstrating their superiority over the other parent.

Throughout your stepchild's life, regular occasions present themselves during which both biological parents and both stepparents will be present. School plays, graduations, ball games, birthday parties, weddings, and baptisms are all occasions when both families may gather to celebrate a special moment in the child's life. It would seem that at such times the focus of celebration ought to be turned upon the child, upon the accomplishment of a significant milestone or noteworthy event in the child's life. Instead, these are often the very occasions when parents give themselves over to bullying, one-upmanship, pride, self-promotion, and just generally counting their own self-image as more important than the child's celebration.

A few years ago, two acquaintances of mine announced their intention to marry. The woman's parents were divorced, and she was their only child. Instead of setting their differences aside in order to celebrate one of the greatest days in the life of their daughter, the parents decided that the wedding and reception would be a great forum for a public contest of hubris. Though the bride and groom preferred a small wedding with a simple but elegant reception, the parents engaged in a battle which degenerated into a glut of spending. That church, though the site of weddings for many wealthy families, had never seen such an elaborate ceremony. The reception, held at a nearby ballroom, was a five-course, seated, champagne dinner for over four hundred guests. Neither family had that level of income, and the bride and groom never desired such extravagance. Unfortunately, their special day was less a celebration of love and a new beginning than it was a rehashing of old animosities and rivalry.

Granted, that wedding was a worst-case scenario, but divorced parents often engage in a public game of one-upmanship. From ball games to baptisms, so many parents choose the public arena to demonstrate a supposed superiority over their ex-spouses—and all to no good end. Children can almost always see through the veneer of self-importance and recognize petty immaturity for precisely what it is. The child is less often impressed, and more often humiliated, by parents who act like strutting adolescents. In such cases, neither parent gains, and the child is always the biggest loser.

Too Many Bosses

One of the most difficult areas for the child to handle is public discipline when four adults to whom the child feels responsible are present. By the time a child with two families reaches elementary school age, the child will have learned (or, in the case of a recently ended marriage, will soon discern) that each family has its own set of behavioral standards and deportment codes. It becomes a very difficult juggling act for the child to determine whose rules are in effect, especially when the child is receiving a constant influx of competing signals from the adults.

The problem may extend far beyond discipline, such as in those cases when the child finds that there are many ways of doing almost anything and that each family believes it has received a special, divine communication of the "right" way. From a father and a stepfather who each insist that they can instruct the peewee leaguer in the best way to approach the kicking tee, to the divorced pair who each is certain that their daughter's hair will only flatter her if cut in that one special way, to the mother who feels fourteen is a good age for dating while the father is certain that his daughter cannot possibly be emotionally ready for a relationship before sixteen—we continuously and conspicuously place our children in situations primed for disaster.

For most of us, our instruction of our children is designed to demonstrate to them that a rationale and objective must precede every decision. When children see their two families making decisions and meting out discipline more for the sake of proving control than for producing desired results, they may come to view the entire decision-making process as arbitrary and irrelevant. Moreover, they will lose faith in both parents as trustworthy and wise counsel. If we choose to make the lives of our children and stepchildren a public contest of wills, such is the risk we must assume.

Then What Do We Do?

Recognizing the difficulty of facing the public does not answer the primary question of this chapter: How do we handle these public encounters? That answer must come on two levels, one applied and one conceptual. On the first level, there are several concrete steps you and your spouse can take to lessen the strain of times when both families are present. At the very least, these steps will take the burden of balancing behavior off the child—and that must be the ultimate objective.

Be open and honest with your children about the difficulty of meeting the public in awkward situations. Children very quickly pick up the signs of tension and discomfort. It is of no benefit to the child to pretend that such situations do not exist. Denial does not make the situation disappear, nor does it provide the social and emotional skills necessary for the child to successfully engage in public interaction.

Whenever possible, we should be proactive rather than reactive in helping our children deal with these encounters. Therefore, in age-appropriate language, you and your spouse should talk to your children about how they should respond in various settings. For adolescent children, general discussion with appropriate specifics will usually meet their needs.

Younger, elementary age children, however, need general, context-setting discussion and specific instruction that will mentally and emotionally prepare them for dealing with particular encounters. This means that, while first talking in general about how to handle these situations so that they are at least somewhat prepared to face the unexpected situation, we should anticipate potentially difficult encounters and talk about our specific responses. We then help the child prepare to be gracious.

Second, establish the rules beforehand with the other family. In Chapter 7, we discuss the dynamics of the relationship between two families who share children. One of the hallmarks of this discussion is the need for communication between the children's divorced parents. Especially in questions of discipline, communication is absolutely essential if both families are to interact successfully in public. Do not "play it by ear" or make up the rules as you go along. The rules must be established beforehand.

Generally speaking, I would suggest that the families agree that, for the purpose of public discipline, the child should receive direction and correction only from the family who is in possession of the child at that time. Actually, from a legal standpoint, in most states only the family with present custody of the child (either from managing conservatorship or present visitation) has the responsibility of parental authority.

Such a surrendering of parental rights is both unnatural and difficult. Parents correctly feel that they should be able to discipline and guide their children in any situation. If only the feelings of the parents were to be considered, the answer would be quite different. Time after time, however, I have seen children find it impossible to answer to two conflicting authorities who maintain different standards of behavior. For the sake of the children, we must move beyond a "They are my children and I will correct them anytime I see fit" mentality and establish an atmosphere of beneficial discipline in which they can become mature and productive adults. Remember, discipline is for the sake of the child, not the parent.

There are, of course, exceptions to this standard. At times, a child needs immediate instruction or assistance, and any proximate adult, but especially a parent, needs to step in. At other times, the possessory parent may choose to relegate or share authority and request that the other parent become involved.

There is always a temptation to flaunt an authority or possessory position in front of the other parent. The children may be allowed to engage publicly in behavior that is anathema to the standards or the beliefs of the other parent. When, by so doing, a parent allows or encourages the child to publicly humiliate the other parent, he or she has entered into a highly volatile and destructive pattern of behavior. When you and your spouse are in charge of your stepchildren in a public setting, you must be constantly sensitive to the concerns of the non-possessory parent. Such a sensitivity must be explicitly discussed with the children. It may very well be that the child learns that, in certain situations, certain behavior that would otherwise be acceptable becomes off-limits because it would offend the other parent. While the temptation is to say, "That is their problem; they can deal with it," it is much more beneficial for the child to learn concern for and sensitivity to the positions of others.

Third, resolve never to initiate the game of one-up-manship and never to rise to the bait that is offered. Few things tempt most divorced individuals more than the opportunity to get in a shot at a former spouse. It enhances a sense of self-worth, it provides a feeling of just retribution, and, ultimately, it is absolutely disastrous for the children of that marriage. Public conflict accomplishes nothing of value. It really does not salve old hurts; the emotional needs of a wounded marriage partner must be addressed in a different context. Indeed, when the child experiences ongoing conflict between his parents, the child's wounds are continually abraded. For the sake of our children, we cannot act like children.

The Response of Grace

Opportunities for success of varying levels appear regularly throughout our lives. This success may entail small personal triumphs—perhaps a high mark on an exam—or significant individual victories whose effects ripple far beyond our own lives—perhaps the composition of a symphony or the consummation of a far-reaching business deal. It seems to me that levels of such opportunity appear in almost everyone's life at some juncture. Why, then, do some people successfully utilize opportunities as springboards for even greater success? Successful people are those who place themselves in the position to take advantage of both positive and negative opportunities that are presented them. They are never caught off guard.

In even a casual reading of the Gospels, one must be struck by Jesus' constant mastery of diverse situations. The religious hierarchy of the day consistently and conspicuously set snares to entrap him. From the story of the woman taken in adultery to the questions following his healing of the lame man, the Pharisees were intent not upon discovering religious truth, but upon forcing Jesus into a violation of the Torah or into a compromise of his principles. Without exception, Jesus' refusal to be caught off guard by these situations allowed him to turn the encounter into a demonstration of his wisdom and integrity.

As in the life of Christ, a clear and sharp distinction exists between reaction to a situation and adaptability within a situation. Adaptability demands that we recognize the ever-present possibility that situations we may encounter are not what we desire them to be. It is incumbent upon us as stepparents that we become comfortable within the tension of situations beyond our control. If, for example, your husband's former wife chooses to direct a not-so-subtle barb toward your parenting skills at a Little League game, you and your husband can respond in kind. By so doing, however, you teach your children that returning as good as you get is the best policy. Or you can refuse to respond in kind, ignoring the dig, and by so doing, teach your children to return good for evil.

Whenever we chart a course of response to the other parents, we take relationships with our spouses and children along for the ride. If we choose a path of vindictiveness and retribution, we are also choosing these options for our families. If, instead, we choose consistently to return good for evil and walk the path of righteousness, our families also join us for that journey.

CHAPTER SIX

Discipline in the Stephome

It is one thing to praise discipline; it is another to submit to it.

—Cervantes

Why does God do things the way he does? It certainly seems it would be much easier for him to act by divine fiat, especially in the related activities of creation and redemption—the very places where we know him best. At the end of each generation, he could wipe everything out and start all over again; that would seem to be the most efficient means of introducing new life. To redeem, he could call people into a relationship with him simply through the activity of his spirit upon their lives.

But God does not work that way. Instead, in both creation and redemption, he involves human activity. He uses human agents—parents—to bring into being the new creation which is formed in his image. And then, he uses human agents—Christians —to call others into relationship with him. Why?

It seems that even a casual reading of Scripture points to the answer. God is all about relationships, and for him, relationships mean a sharing of responsibility. The whole story of the Garden and dominion over creation is a statement that God intends for us to be co-creators with him. Even his most precious gift of salvation he entrusts to us. In the book of Ephesians Paul says, "I have received a stewardship of God's grace" (RSV). That is, he intimates that we have been trusted with God's greatest gift and with the responsibility of sharing that gift with others. In no place is this sacred trust more evident than in a family relationship where God has delivered to parents children created in the image of the Divine.

A theology of the family, then, begins with an understanding of this gift of God. As parents, our concept of familial roles, discipline in the home, and child rearing in general begins when we understand that God has chosen to share with us what he could have claimed as his divine prerogative.

Learning the Relationship

In most first marriages, the marriage partners are young enough still to be shaping their ideas concerning many of life's most important issues. One of the advantages of an early marriage is that the husband and wife form these concepts and ideas together, forging a reasonably homogeneous household. Because they are formed in concert, the family's standards are a matter of joint conviction rather than compromise between the partners' ideals. Thus, parents are usually able to speak with one voice on most issues. Conversely, second marriages generally occur after values, ideals, and convictions have already been established. Therefore, both the mother and the father must seek areas of common ground, points of compromise, and proximate means of reaching goals in order to make family life a success. To do so almost always takes a very concerted effort. In no area is such exertion and diligence more needed than in the question of discipline.

The Bible is replete with instructions, both implicit and explicit, for parents to discipline their children. This biblical mandate is given from a perspective that wise and careful discipline is a means of expressing love by assuring the future well-being of the child. This perspective says that the child's long-term spiritual, emotional, and physical health is more important than immediate and temporal discomfort. Such a view demands discipline not only of the child, but also of the parent.

Christian homes, by and large, agree that the biblical calls for discipline are to be heeded. There is less unanimity, however, as to the form and method of the discipline. Few areas in the Christian home can bring more stress and damage to the husband/wife relationship than can questions concerning proper methodology for disciplining the child. Those questions must find resolution.

Shifting Values and Floating Standards

Most of us like to believe that we practice value-based behavior; that is, our activities reflect deeply held beliefs. We tell the truth because we believe that deceit is morally wrong; we practice monogamy because we understand that adulterous violation of the marriage relationship transgresses divine intent; we do not steal because we understand the right to property is God-given. Our values, be they positive or negative, determine the way we function in familial and societal relationships, although, in almost everyone's life, there is a gap between ideal values and actual behavior. Even so, these values nonetheless serve as a foundation and building blocks for our character and identity.

Values are not developed in a vacuum; they are almost always learned in relationships. For most of us, the foundational values are established in our childhood home, with our parents and siblings. These values are refined and amended in the early years of adulthood, usually in the first marriage. One of the most difficult voyages for a young couple is the journey to establishing common values, and the initial years of marriage are usually spent designing the common-ground beliefs that will shape behavior in the years to come.

Establishing value patterns in a second marriage is even more difficult. If children are present, the husband and wife do not have the luxury of seeking out common ground over a period of years. Instead, they are immediately called upon to work out new ways of relating and making value judgments within an already established context.

The difficulty begins because of our perception of the nature of values. Ironically, in the Christian family, where it would seem that the commonality of values would be a given, the establishment of shared values can be an even more daunting task. Especially for those of us who have been active in church and Christian activities throughout our lives, there is the feeling that our values reflect not only what we believe but the divine intent for all persons. Therefore, a disagreement with a Christian spouse concerning a value, or even a standard of behavior, becomes not only a behavioral issue but a challenge to the validity of our understanding of God's will. For the Christian couple, finding common ground in values may mean the surrender of behavioral patterns, attitudes, and even beliefs that are a part of our Christian identity.

In such areas, the Christian stepparent must tread very carefully. The three keys to dealing with challenges to values are *honesty, integrity,* and *humility.* The first of these, honesty, is primarily a self-focus; that is, we must honestly recognize value conflicts and the sources of these conflicts. Second, in a stepfamily relationship, integrity in communication and discussion of value conflicts is absolutely essential. As a stepparent, you must have the moral integrity to discuss openly with your husband or wife the challenges that arise from conflict in values. Finally—and this is probably the most important—the stepparent must have the humility to recognize that what has been a deeply held value, a conviction of moral right, may in actuality be a personal preference. It is of utmost importance in a marriage relationship that each spouse give the partner the respect and freedom to be a moral player in his or her own right. My values may not be your values, but that does not necessarily make them wrong.

Any doctrine of sin begins with the recognition that knowledge and insight are limited—Paul's "through a glass darkly"—and, therefore, the perspective of your spouse has an equivalent *prima facie* validity to your own. My wife is just as likely to be right as I am. A solid parenting relationship begins with respect for the other's viewpoint.

Accepting a spouse's right to opinion, of course, does not finally lay to rest the question of establishing standards when the stepparent genuinely feels that the parent has adopted values that are either morally wrong or not in the best interest of the children. In such cases, the stepparent is called upon to tread very carefully. If you decide that a specific area of conflict leaves no room for moral tolerance, and feel a need to take a stand, that stand must be taken very measuredly and with total awareness of possible consequences.

One woman tells the story of stepchildren who had an absolutely different value system than she did: They had no respect for the property rights of others. Her stepchildren stole from her, from her husband, and from other people. It came to a point where she was afraid to take them shopping because of constant shoplifting, which was approaching kleptomania. When she confronted her husband, he shrugged it off with a "boys will be boys" comment. She did not feel that way. She recognized this as a moral wrong that could, and probably would, lead to serious character damage to the children. And she took a stand: such behavior had no place in her family.

Even in a case like that, however, the means of taking the stand must be carefully measured. A judgmental air, a "this is the way it has to be done," a "my way or the highway" approach will be more likely to get the highway than the desired moral return. When the family is already adjusting to new personalities and environments, a value adjustment comes only with great difficulty.

Therefore, the bringing of new values into a family is to be undertaken with an air of love and with absolute nonjudgmentalism on the character of the person(s) involved. Instead, the focus rests upon the act rather than the actor.

Who Disciplines When?

Neil Diamond's autobiographical anthem "I Am, I Said" depicts a man struggling not only to claim his identity but to have others also recognize his value and worth as a person. So it often goes for the stepparent. While searching to gain understanding of who we are in our relationship with our children, we are often, at the same time, seeking respect and honor from those children. At times we force ourselves on them, demanding emotional intimacy, the deference due a parent, and full status as a primary care provider. We may not replace the child's biological parent, but we want all of the rights and privileges thereof.

The adults in the family must find a mechanism by which they may relate to one another and to the children and yet maintain an orderly household, a household in which the children can grow up to become productive members of society. To do so means that the parents must define their roles—not only with each other, but also in relation to the children—because, like it or not, the stepparent must have a disciplinary role with the children. The stepparent may not be the primary agent of discipline, or even a co-equal in that area, but he or she is nonetheless a vital player on a child's discipline team. Establishing the parenting role demands that both the parent and the stepparent identify the manner in which the stepparent will make the transition into the discipline role. As a prerequisite, there must be an establishment of house rules, value systems, and expectations.

A colleague tells the story of her first encounter with her new stepfamily. She met and developed a relationship with her future spouse which grew into a commitment before she had the chance to introduce herself to his family. She traveled several hundred miles from her home to spend a weekend getting to know her future stepdaughters. By nature a very organized and tidy individual, she was led by her husband-to-be through the threshold of what was to become their home. She was greeted not only by his enthusiastic teenage daughter, but also by an unkempt house—piles of clothes and unwashed dishes. Her future stepdaughter established the agenda very quickly: "We're so glad you're here; we so very much needed someone to clean up this place." It was a matter of some time after their marriage before she could convince her family that a clean house was a family effort, not a mother's responsibility.

Any stepparent finds it difficult to transform the "yours and mine" into "ours." For the planned merger, no area looms more threateningly than does the question of discipline. Many families are never able to deal with the most critical family issue of all: how they will deal with disciplining each other's children. When the partners bring in different values and standards of behavior, as well as different methodological concepts about disciplining children, the marriage is ripe for some serious difficulty.

Take, for example, a family in which the stepfather

appears as the strict disciplinarian whereas the mother of the children believes in freedom and independence. The stepfather may determine that yelling, cajoling, or immediate punishment is the best way to have his family "shape up." He expects the children to do what they are told, when they are told to do it, and to measure up to what he believes is right, not what they may think is best for them. At the same time, the mother, believing that individuality is a hallmark of a healthy child, allows them to set many of their own standards for schoolwork, room cleanliness, and relationships with others.

In such cases, what will inevitably result will be undermined parental authority, conflict between the parents, and a confused child. The stepfather may intercede to correct what he sees as a problem in behavior, perhaps acting too rashly and coming down on the child too strongly. The mother, uncomfortable with the outburst, steps in and tries to soften the blow. In so doing, however, she brings herself—in front of the children—into conflict with her husband. At that point, the child is looking for—and finds—a way to escape the discipline the stepfather has tried to impose.

What happens in such a scenario is that neither parent recognizes the primary role that raising the children occupies in the stepfamily. Instead, they have falsely assumed that they can move naturally into their own roles in the family, and everything will "just work out." Discipline in the stephome requires that both parent and stepparent come to agreement on methods and standards. Refusal to do so courts disaster.

Some psychologists and sociologists suggest that the stepparent is to have no role in the discipline of the children. I strongly disagree. Inevitably the stepparent will become involved in the rearing of the children, especially in the custodial home. When the stepparent and the child are constantly around each other, the stepparent must have the explicitly expressed authority to discipline and correct the child.

The question, instead, is over how *large* a role the stepparent is to play. This decision must be related to each family's particular situation, especially in relationship to the age of the children. Just as in the effective telling of a joke, "timing is everything," timing both in the life of the stepchild and in the life of the marriage. The prominence of the role of disciplinarian for the stepparent is inversely proportional to the first and directly proportional to the second. That is, the older the child is at the time of the marriage, the less involved in discipline the stepparent can be. And the longer the stepparent has been in the child's life, the greater the stepparent's role in discipline will be.

If a stepfather walks into the life of a teenager and immediately begins to lay down hard and fast rules, the teenager, already wrestling to control rampaging adolescent hormones and trying to stretch his wings to freedom, will have nothing but a negative reaction to the stepparent's attempt to exert authority. We all, of course, have heard stories and examples to the contrary: the stepfather who walks into the out-of-control teenage son's life and with a quick and firm hand sets him back on the straight and narrow.

Such cases happen. They are, however, the exception rather than the rule. When a stepparent tries to force his or her authority upon a teenage child, the answer is much more likely to be rebellion than redemption. In such situations, the stepparent almost certainly benefits the child and their relationship more by seeking to be special counsel and friend, which can never occur if the first thing the child sees you do is flex your muscles of parental authority.

Conversely, the longer the stepparent has been a part of the family, the greater is not only the "right" but also the ability to function as a disciplinarian. The stepparent who walks into any child's life, no matter what the age of the child, with the pronouncement (audible or otherwise) "I'm here and I'm in charge" is asking for trouble. The ability to discipline must not be mistaken for permission to keep the children in line. Those are two totally different concepts.

The basic premise of discipline is that children through guidance, instruction, example, and correction learn an acceptable and approved way to relate to themselves, to others, to God, and to the environment. Such learning demands a level of trust that is not won overnight. When the child begins to see you are consistent with the values you espouse, the behavior you expect, and the standards you establish, then true discipline can occur.

Note the biblical injunction: "Train up a child in the way he should go, / And when he is old he will not depart from it" (Prov. 22:6). This is not a demand that we keep our children in line so that they do not bother or embarrass us or so that we can show who is boss. Rather, the emphasis is on establishing a relationship that allows the children to see you as the kind of person you want them to become. Modeling that type of life demands discipline not only for the children but also for the parent. Genuine discipline is a reciprocal act within the bounds of a relationship. Bullying is an act of insecurity; discipline is an act of love.

The Same Team on the Same Field

The demands of discipline in the home mean that the parent and the stepparent must devise a coherent and consistent child-raising system in which the children can perceive the necessary consistency, love, and standards. In any family, the children need to see that the parents are unified and that they maintain consistent standards. This is even more true in the stepfamily. Children in the stepfamily have already gone through a violent disruption of their lives when their parents were divorced. They underwent a second major change when a new parent—you—walked into their lives. Even more so than children in traditional families, your stepchildren need to see consistent behavior established for them. They do not need to see a parent and a stepparent fighting over how the children should behave.

The establishment of a consistent discipline pattern must, to some extent, be agreed upon before the marriage; of necessity, however, a great deal of the discipline focus can only develop, as a scientist would say, *en vivo*. As much as it is possible, the parent and the stepparent should, before the wedding, agree upon who will discipline in what situation, appropriate forms of discipline, appropriate levels of discipline, and general objectives for the discipline in the family. At the same time, the couple must be flexible enough to recognize that patterns and agendas are changed by the family's life situation.

Sociologists have defined four general discipline patterns in the stepfamily. In the first pattern, the "your kid, your problem" pattern, the stepparent is absolutely uninvolved with parenting and disciplining the child. In such a case, the stepparent's primary relationship is with the spouse. The stepparent may develop a relationship with the children, but that relationship is more that of a stepsibling (and, thereby, one who has no authority in the relationship) than it is a stepparent. Eventually, however, when the discipline problems that all families go through arise, the stepparent will often feel a great deal of resentment toward the children, especially if the stepparent perceives that he or she is providing a home for the child yet receiving none of the benefits of parenthood. This resentment will almost always damage the relationship between stepparent and stepchild and eventually between husband and wife.

In the second pattern, the "not with my kids you don't" pattern, the stepparent attempts to assume authority that neither the parent nor the stepchild has granted. When the stepparent tries to discipline the child, the parent will interject and inform the stepparent that the primary relationship, the one that has been around since the child's birth, will take care of the problem, and that the stepparent needs to kindly remove himself from the situation.

This family pattern will consistently prevent the stepfamily from integrating and genuinely becoming a family. The stepparent's opinion on any matter, not just on questions of discipline, will almost always be unimportant to the children because the opinions on discipline have been so severely denigrated and rebuked. Again, the relationship between stepparent and stepchild will deteriorate, followed almost certainly by the relationship between the marriage partners.

The third pattern that emerges is the "you deal with it, I'm tired of it" syndrome, which occurs when the parent abdicates parenting responsibility to the stepparent. This pattern almost always occurs when the parent is the opposite sex of the child. A mother may say to a new stepfather, "I've tried to discipline him, and I cannot. You give it a shot." Or a father may say to a new stepmother, "I do not understand teenage girls. See what you can do with them."

When the stepparent then steps in, the child will usually rebel and resent the intrusion. A cycle has been established in which the stepparent tries to get tougher, the child rebels more, and behavioral problems follow. In this pattern, from the child's perspective, the child is forced to deal not only with the loss of a biological parent through the desertion of divorce, but also with the loss of the other biological parent through abdication of the parental role to the stepparent. The stepparent, forced into the parenting role, does not become the new parent for the child, but rather the evil substitute of the Cinderella story.

Only the fourth pattern, the "we're all in this boat together" pattern, integrates the family. Not only do parent and stepparent act in concert, agreeing beforehand as much as possible on principles and standards for the family, but the children are also brought into the decision-making loop. They are allowed to understand that their new stepparent will be taking a progressively larger role in the discipline in the family. They are encouraged to discuss questions of standards, behavior, and expectations with the new stepparent. At the same time, the stepparent earns the right to discipline by modeling a consistent and attractive Christlike behavior in front of the children. As the relationship grows, so does the discipline role of the stepparent. If this model becomes operative in the family, the chances for the survival and the mental and emotional health of the stepfamily are greatly increased.

The Special Challenge of Discipline in the Blended Family

The adjustment to the new rules of the game are difficult even when only a stepparent has been added to the equation. But if a subsequent marriage is required to factor not only stepparent/stepchild relationships, but also stepsibling relationships, the equation becomes immeasurably more complicated.

The basic principles for handling this context will remain the same as when only a stepparent is being added to a family, but two important methodological rules must amend the procedures. First, there must not be two sets of rules for the household. In other words, the standards of the home apply to the entire home. The father cannot establish one set of rules that apply only to his children and the mother establish a second set that apply only to her children. Instead, both parents, in concert with the children, must establish the rules that are applicable to both sets of children.

I am familiar with some homes in which it was decided

that, for all intents and purposes, only the man and woman were getting married; they would maintain separate relationships with their children. In one such home, as it worked out, she had quite different and more restrictive standards for her children than the husband had for his. It was not long at all before chaos was the only working rule in the home. Her children wanted to know why the other kids were allowed to "get away with murder," while they were held to a higher standard. His kids were constantly worried that their stepmother's tough standards would eventually be applied to them. The children grew to resent each other, and the home was in constant turmoil.

The relationships that should have been growing and healthy were retarded and stunted in their growth. When unequal standards are applied, children quickly grow to perceive that the rules and standards in the home are completely arbitrary without any basis in a higher morality or standard. So they will feel justified in violating them whenever their personal desires lead them to believe that to be the best course of action. It is a situation tailor-made for disaster.

The second standard is closely related to the first: When the new rules are established, they should represent a fair blending of the rules of the two families. If one family walks in and pronounces "This is the way we have always done it, and this is the way we will continue to do it," and by so doing expects the other family to surrender their way of doing things, it sends a message that the other family's values and standards and, consequently, the family members, are of little worth in the new relationship. Immediately, a dynamic is established whereby one family is inherently superior to the other. Again, a situation is formed in which the reconstituted family will be at war with itself.

Instead, through premarital conversations between first the parents and then the full families, the new household rules should be established. Many of these, of a certainty, will have to be amended and the course will be slightly corrected throughout the life of the relationship, but the family needs a clear picture of the larger principles as the relationships are founded. When the rules are laid out beforehand, the children are much less likely to accuse the parents of unfairness or partiality.

Discipline by Moments

Only a few months after Susan and I married, my first-grade stepdaughter came walking down the hall with the world globe, wanting to know the location of Iraq and who this "Saddam Hussein guy" was. Although at that time I was involved in helping sort clothes for the wash, she and I curled up amidst the piles of laundry with her globe and began looking at the Middle East and talking about the problems that had developed there since biblical times. A chance was even provided to talk about how people will often invoke the "will of God" for actions that have nothing to do with divine intent and everything to do with personal lust and greed. Somehow, there surrounded by mounds of clothes for the wash, discussing a question that, to a large extent, was well over the head of a six-year-old, we connected and found a level of emotional intimacy, respect, and trust that we had not known before. In such moments does discipline find its genesis.

If discipline is less about punishment than it is about helping a child to discover appropriate biblical standards of moral behavior, by modeling, by the child's learning trust, by punishment when necessary—then we must be quick to capture the moments when the relationship of trust can be enhanced. So doing requires that we are ever diligent and constantly aware that what worked one time, what was the best punishment one time, and what was the best reward another time may not be appropriate in every situation.

At times in every relationship, but certainly in a parent/child and especially in a stepparent/stepchild relationship, a new route or a new angle of approach must be taken. Occasionally, you—or even your spouse, but not both of you at the same time—may need to back out of the correction business for awhile. If it has become a contest of wills rather than a lesson in morality, perhaps the other adult in the home should handle it for awhile. That may be tough on your ego, but it may be the right thing to do. Raising children to become what God has designed them to be is not a matter of showing them who is boss. It is a matter of respecting them as you require respect from them, of hearing them as you demand that they listen to you, and of responding to their needs as you insist upon obedience in their behavior.

CHAPTER
SEVEN

The
Other Side

Gee, two dads; just like the television show.
—a child commenting on another child's
father and stepfather

A few years ago the daughter of good friends experienced a divorce. It was a particularly brutal parting of ways. Without warning, her husband left her—but not before emptying the bank account, taking the furniture, and cruelly calling her at work to tell her she needed to check on the house that afternoon because he was going to be gone for awhile. She went home from work to find an empty home and a devastated life. He had disappeared without a trace. The next time anyone heard from him he was having legal trouble in another state and looking for help.

At the time all this happened, this young woman's mother said to me, "It would have been so much easier if he had just died." She was right. If he had been killed in an auto accident, there would have been insurance money to collect; there would have been no feelings of desertion or failure; there would not have been the stigma of divorce. There would have been a time of grieving, but no time of embarrassment. As it was, he left a wife now considered "unclean" by many members of her church family. He left pain and anger and a wonderful woman with very little to show for her years of effort in trying to hold the marriage together.

The young lady's mother was not wishing that he was dead, though many mothers of a so-wronged daughter would. Rather, she only recognized that a death might require less healing than the divorce. Has there ever been a father or a mother, divorced from their child's other parent, who has not entertained thoughts that it would be much easier if the former spouse were, if not dead, at least completely out of the picture? Even at its very best—when both families share the same objectives and goals for their children, when parents agree on the spending of the child support check, when each biological parent genuinely believes that the other biological parent has the child's best interest in mind—even in those situations the relationship between two actively involved parental families in a child's life is extremely difficult.

Let's restate the obvious: Marriages end in divorce because of conflict. Were it not for conflict, there would be few divorces. Studies reveal that, second only to financial problems, disagreement over child rearing is the number one cause of divorce. There is no reason to think that those differences will disappear simply because a judge issues a divorce decree and gives custody of the children to one or both of the parents. Unless one parent has chosen—or has had the choice made for them—to be absent either physically, emotionally, or both from the child's life, conflict is inevitable. The question has never been whether or not there will be conflict. The question always has been and always will be how disagreements between a child's divorced biological parents can be managed in a manner that is most conducive to the well-being of the child.

We all want an environment that is as normal as possible for our children. For most of us, "normal" means a two-parent family, free from outside interference, producing a healthy environment that allows the children to grow to emotional, physical, and spiritual maturity with as few disruptions as possible.

By definition, the stepfamily is not such a place. One of the parents with whom the child lives is not the biological parent. In a solid majority of stepfamily situations, the non-managerial, biological parent is still in the child's life either through support payments, visitation rights, involvement in the decision-making process, and/or involvement at varying levels in the child's upbringing. The "normal" family schedule cannot be maintained. Summers are disrupted by periods of visitation, perhaps only half of the weekends are available for your family, even family dinners may be regularly interrupted by the evening call from Mom or Dad. It seems life would be a lot easier if the other side . . . Then perhaps we could live a normal life with our children and stepchildren.

But would this price of normalcy be in the best interest of the children? Almost certainly not. As difficult as the presence of the non-managerial parent may make life for us (or for that manner, the managerial presence if your spouse does not have custody of the children), the absence of that mother or father is far more damaging to the child. Psychologists tell us that, in those families where a parent has chosen to absent himself from the child's life, the child will frequently suffer lifelong emotional scars of such rejection. The exception to this, of course, may be those families in which the child was too young at the time of separation to remember the absent parent. The preservation of your child's emotional health, even in the midst of the turmoil that two-family parenting brings, is well worth the price you are forced to pay for dealing with the constant distraction of the other side. What is most important is that you and your spouse learn to deal competently with the difficulty of the situation and that, through example and instruction, your children learn how to deal with the same situations.

Carrying Baggage

Let's restate the obvious again: Your spouse is no longer married to his or her ex-wife or -husband. Unfortunately, however, it seems that many divorced individuals never learn that different rules apply to a relationship between husband and wife and a relationship between ex-spouses. In the vast majority of divorce cases, some level of emotional abuse is evident. While we will all acknowledge that such mistreatment is wrong, nonetheless, this feature is common to most troubled marriages. When the marriage ends, however, much tighter strictures are placed upon one's individual "right" to emotionally—usually verbally—attack their ex-spouse. While shouting may have been the standard method of communication in the marriage, it has absolutely no place between divorced individuals. It is not an approved means of communication.

At the same time, neither must baggage left over from

the dissolution of the marriage be carried either overtly or secretly into discussions concerning the upbringing of the children. A divorced friend blames her husband—rightly—for the breakup of their marriage and "destroying my life." She is right; he was wrong. He behaved in a manner that would destroy even the strongest of marriages, and theirs did not have solid footing from the beginning.

They are now divorced, and it is critically important that she learn to put the animosities and her feelings of betrayal behind her as they "negotiate" the future of the children. Instead, she has constantly used the children as a vehicle for punishing her ex-husband for what he did to her. She inadvertently "forgets" to give the children mail from their father. They are always unavailable when he calls, and she (in violation of the state statutes) often denies him visitation privileges. Unfortunately, she has misread the bigger picture. Her adversary is not the one injured. The ones being punished in such a situation are the children, even more than the ex-husband.

We must understand that our children are not a battleground upon which the hostilities of the previous marriage can be trampled. It is amazing how many divorced couples who were so careful to shield the children from the conflict going on in the home and to make sure the children understood that they were not responsible for the divorce nonetheless allow the children to become the arena of ongoing conflict.

Divorced couples must find a mechanism by which they can get beyond the hostilities and anger of the divorce, especially when they are dealing with the children. Your, or your husband's or wife's, baggage is not to be strapped to the back of the children. Don't make them carry it.

The Right to Participate

Perspective is everything, and we are almost always limited to seeing only our view. In the case of a divorced couple, the perspectives of the managerial parent and the non-managerial parent concerning rights and intrusions rarely meet. A managerial mother may claim, "You're the one who left," while the father may say, "I divorced you, not the children." Who is right?

Both. The father (and we use the father only as an example, not suggesting that the man is usually at fault) can rightly contend that the conflict was between him and his wife, not between him and the children. Thereby, he rightly feels that this conflict should have as little effect as possible on his relationship with the children. He may not be able, if the mother has custody, to be in their lives each day, but he is nonetheless their father and still has all the rights and responsibilities thereof.

At the same time, the mother may claim, "I didn't ask for any of this" or "I didn't seek the divorce; I didn't leave. He may still be their father, but why should *his* choice affect *my* relationship with my children? I didn't want the divorce. Why should I now have to give up half of my summers? I didn't ask him to leave. Why do I have to have my weekend schedule interrupted every month?"

Both parents have absolutely valid positions, but both positions are incompatible. Therefore, what this means is, although you may be right and your ex-spouse may have a logical or legally valid standpoint in asserting his or her rights, such assertion is going to accomplish nothing. At that point, both families must act in grace. Each family must recognize—and hopefully empathize with—the other family's position. One parent wants to see no disruption at all, feeling that they are not to blame. The other sees no reason to tie the relationship with the children to fault in the divorce. Both are legitimate; therefore, there must be a meeting in the middle.

The problem occurs, however, when one family is willing to recognize the reality of the conflicting positions and the legitimacy of both views and the other family is not. At that point, we return to the paradigm we discussed in Chapter 2: have a strong back but a willing heart; search for ways to accommodate both families. Do not run from conflict out of fear, but seek to minimize disputes for the well-being of everyone involved. A non-custodial parent has both the right and the obligation to be involved in the important choices in the child's life. Major decisions should be discussed between both parents, and the managerial parent must give weight to the wants and wishes of the child's other biological parent because ultimately the moral and ethical responsibility for the upbringing of the child still belongs to both parents. At the same time, however, the non-managerial parent must recognize the legal responsibility that the managerial parent has to make choices affecting the physical, social, and religious upbringing of the child. While the laws vary from state to state, by and large those decisions ultimately rest with the managerial parent.

Only by recognizing the rights—both God-given and state-awarded—of the other parent can an atmosphere conducive to the well-being of the child be established. Both biological parents should have the same agenda, at least in the larger context. They should want to see their children grow up to be healthy physically, mentally, socially, and spiritually. Once that is recognized, the methodological difficulties can be overcome. That means one biological parent has to give the other the benefit of the doubt. If it is at all possible, always operate on the assumption that the ex-spouse really does have the child's best interest at heart. That interest may get clouded or may even be obscured by self-interest at times, but nonetheless, down there somewhere both families are working for the same end. As long as that goal is kept before the families, the difficulties can be overcome.

Acting in Integrity

One difficult situation the stepfamily faces in dealing with the other side is when one family attempts to damage the child's relationship with the other family by denigrating that family in front of the child. The cases are all too common in which a father or a mother chooses to attack an ex-spouse through the child. Such attacks usually are a result of a parent's insecurity; when a parent feels that his or her relationship with the child is threatened, the most tempting solution is to downplay the worth of the other parent. Choices that have been made for the children are criticized, attacks on intelligence are offered, or the worth of the other parent as a person is impugned.

It is interesting to note that even more than relations within the stepfamily, the stepfamily's well-being is often based upon the manner in which the non-custodial parent accepts the new stepfamily and is accepted by it. As we have noted throughout, husbands and wives divorce each other but not their children; therefore, the ex-spouse remains an integral part of the dynamics of the stepfamily. To some extent, without regard to the presence or absence of the non-custodial parent, there remains continual interaction between the biological parent, the stepparent, and the children on one hand and the non-custodial parent on the other hand.

Very often the stepparent has the most trouble dealing with the relationship; the stepparent may view the other biological parent as a threat and enter into a jealous competition with him or her. Conversely, if an open, honest, and healthy relationship with the other parent is developed, that interaction can become foundational to a healthy stepfamily. If the children, in their interaction with the two families, are able to see that loyalty to one parent is not inimical to loyalty to the other parent, they are not called upon to question their own identity or family values. Instead, they can accept nurture and love from both families and grow and mature within the context of these healthy relationships.

Conflict often develops between the stepparent and the same sex parent, perhaps from jealousy on the parent's part and/or envy on the stepparent's part. The stepparent may envy the fact that he or she is not the child's biological parent. They may be called upon to fulfill all the functions of "parent" by providing a home, discipline, financial support, and love. They may have to be there for the child through both the good times and the bad; therefore, the stepparent becomes envious of the biological parent's identity as the "real parent." At the same time, the biological parent may fear an intrusion by the stepparent and jealously guard those parental prerogatives. When the parent sees a growing affection and a growing relationship between the child and the stepparent, the parent may fear being shut out of the child's life, and resentment toward the stepparent will grow.

Both the envy and the jealousy stem from a denial of the reality of the stepfamily. The custodial parent, the children, and the stepparent may desire to replace the broken family with a brand new one that is identical to the biological family in every respect. Instead of accepting that they are a binuclear family, they try to become the new nuclear family with the correlative one set of parents.

At the same time, the non-resident, biological parent also does not recognize that a stepfamily *is* different from the nuclear family and that the nuclear family, in this case, no longer exists. He or she may still want all the rights and prerogatives of a parent and may not want to share the children with anyone.

Again, denial of the reality of the stepfamily prevents a successful communication. Such competition has two basic ingredients. The first is the perception of misplaced rights, and the second, a wounded ego. Both of these are clearly present in the dynamic of the two family relationships that comprise the modern stepfamily.

This competition commonly forces itself to the forefront in two ways. First, and probably the most common, is that one parent will constantly defame the other parent to the children. Interestingly enough, most parents usually claim to do this in the best interest of the children so that they "will really understand what your dad (or mom) is like."

Make no mistake about it. Attacks on and defamation of the character of the other parent has absolutely nothing to do with the well-being of the children, and we must recognize that. It has everything to do with our own lack of self-esteem and our own jealousy or envy of the relationship between child and parent. What parent would not want her or his children to have a positive relationship with both parents and feel good about the relationships? That would almost seem to be a given.

Unfortunately, however, an amazingly high percentage of divorced couples find it necessary to use the children for a battleground to vent their own feelings of inadequacy. Ultimately, such attacks do no good for either parent. Children, even young elementary school children, are quick to see through such attacks and recognize their phoniness. Conversely, when we refuse to rise to attack, when we don't "take the bait," our refusal to return evil for evil will reap its rewards. Children can look at their parents and understand that it is not necessary to get in the gutter just because someone else is there. They can look at the restrained parents and recognize the dignity and character that they possess.

It is especially important that custodial parents do not defame the absent parent. As we have discussed before, children tend to idealize the parent who is not there; the absent parent is always the "perfect" one. When the present parent attacks the character and worth of the absent parent, the child is forced to either reject out of hand the pronouncement of the present parent, thus losing all trust and respect he has for that parent, or to dichotomize his image of the absent parent into the wonderful things he believes about that parent and the terrible things that the custodial parent says about them. Either way, all parties involved lose.

Setting the Agenda

In most stepfamily situations, both parents feel a natural need to control and to set the agenda for the child's life. To pronounce the level of control and the person who controls, however, is often a matter of conflict between the two families. Most child psychologists suggest that a child needs to understand that one family is ultimately responsible for him, and that responsibility exists no matter whom the child is with. Dr. Albert Solnit goes as far as suggesting that joint custody could never be the best arrangement for the child. The child needs to know that one family is responsible for the child, and the child is responsible to that family.

The parent who, during the time of summer or weekend visitation, intentionally undercuts the authority of the custodial parent with pronouncements such as "forget what your father says; you're with me now, and his rules don't apply" undermines the trust relationship between parent and child. The child should not have one set of rules for the week and a new set for the weekend. The child should not be taught during the school year that some things are morally wrong and then in the summer be told "we do that all the time, and there's nothing wrong with it." The parents must communicate. When the child is of elementary school age, such inconsistencies are landmines that are destined to explode during the years of adolescent rebellion. Although it may salve a wounded ego and build up damaged self-esteem, a parent's insistence on ignoring the standards of the other parent can be absolutely devastating for the child.

What, then, can be the role in authority and discipline of the non-custodial parent? When it is under-stood that the assertion of rights with a "they're my kids, and I'll teach them as I please" attitude is extremely dangerous for the child's emotional and mental health, the non-custodial parent must search for ways to com-municate—sometimes forcefully—concern, desires, and objectives for the child to the custodial parent. Granted, that method of raising children is fraught with frustration, but semi-annual or annual conferences with open and honest discussion about the state of the child must be held.

The non-custodial parent has an obligation to express opinions on the way things have gone and the way things ought to be done in the future, and the custodial parent has an obligation to give weight to those concerns. Just hearing them and entertaining them out of politeness is not enough; instead, both must recognize the parental right of the non-custodial parent and incorporate those designs for the child into his or her own. At that level of compromise and cooperation, the hope for a healthy child is born.

Communicating

Nothing is more effective or more difficult than an honest and open face-to-face discussion between the two parents and (depending on the situation) the steppar-ents. If necessary, an outside arbitrator can be brought in, but open conversation is the only proper way to resolve the issues between the two families. I know of several stepmothers who, by and large with good intent, have decided that handwritten correspondence would be a really good way to clear the air between them and their husbands' former wives. These letters usually deal with issues of control, attacks on the family, manipulation of the children, and other assorted unpleasantries, and they almost always accomplish absolutely nothing.

Resist the temptation to take care of the problems by writing. At times correspondence may be appropriate: to let the other parent know of plans, to make sure there is a written record of some incident. But a letter is not the place to deal with hostilities. Such letters usually engender more of that with which they were sent to deal: increased hostility, increased resentment. To a person who has already been involved in attacks, who already thinks evil of the other parties, an additional letter will only serve to confirm the rightness of the anger that already exists.

Instead, schedule regular times of discussion, times when the families can openly and honestly talk about their agendas and hopes for the child. To do so not only clears the air but also allows the children to see that the parents are communicating—they will not be manipulated behind one another's back—and that the parents are big enough to work out differences. Such demonstration is one of the greatest gifts you can provide for your children.

The Child Support Check

Few things in the relationship between stepfamilies engender more conflict than the child support check. Child support represents a legislative recognition that both the managerial and the non-managerial parent have not only rights but also obligations toward the child or children. In most states, by law, that check is given specifically to meet the material welfare needs of the child. In the overwhelming majority of cases where child support is ordered, child support payments are made by the father. This is because the mother usually receives custody of the children, and also, in the cases where the mother does not receive custody, the father nonetheless has the better-paying job and is able to meet the material needs of the children and, therefore, does not receive support from the mother.

The conflict over the use of the child support check can occur for several reasons. Besides the obvious issue of nonsupport which is always an area of controversy, many much more innocent situations can lead to disagreement between the two parties. The first of these occurs simply because the managerial family wants to maintain its financial privacy from the parent who writes the child support check. Resultingly, when the parent writes the child support check and then sees the other family, especially the parents, spending money in a manner he thinks is "unwise" or is a poor use of money, he is quick to assume that the expenditure was made possible by the child support they worked so hard to provide. In reality, the activities may be financed completely differently, and the child support check may in fact be spent quite wisely and specifically for the children's well-being. Nonetheless, the conflict is there.

The second area in which conflict arises comes from disagreement over what "spending for the child's well-being" may be. Most judges who have jurisdiction in child custody cases indicate that they understand that the law does not mandate the child support be spent specifically on the child. In other words, making sure the child has a roof over his or her head (rent or house payments), electricity, and ample food at mealtimes are every bit as legitimate a child support expenditure as are new clothes and recreation. Nonetheless, some fathers get very upset when they do not see their child wearing a new outfit every time they put their signature on a check.

Conversely, an additional area of conflict occurs when the managerial parent feels that the child support check from the non-managerial parent is insufficient and then observes an extravagance in the lifestyle of the non-present parent which she cannot afford to provide for her own children. In such cases, the mother may feel that the father is wanting the privileges of parenthood without accepting the responsibilities thereof.

How then do you deal with conflicts concerning the use of child support? There is an easy answer, but it is one that few families can afford. Whenever possible, the child support check can be immediately deposited in a child's college fund; in other words, do not spend the money but save it for the future use of the college-age child. Doing so will often settle any dispute over use of the funds. We must recognize, however, that such a plan is not feasible for a significant majority of families. The child support check is often essential to pay electric bills and to buy food and clothing for the children. In such cases, it is nonetheless wise to put a consistent monthly percentage of that check into some type of savings program for the child. That not only helps to secure the child's future, but it also demonstrates to the one writing the check that you are making a serious attempt to use the money provided wisely and for the child's benefit.

We recognize, however, that doing so does not alleviate all the problems. The best solution is, of course, to be as open and honest as possible about the way the money is used. It may be an eye-opening experience for both parents to look together at the actual costs of raising children. A 1993 U.S. Department of Agriculture report stated that in 1992 it cost the average family $19,000 per year to support two children. If the two parents are equally bearing the burden of support, that comes out to $4,750 that each family would contribute to raising one child each year. A more extravagant lifestyle would, of course, cost more, and certainly a family could cut down on that amount, but that at least is an indication of what it costs to raise a child today.

Perhaps the best thing that can be done to address concerns about the use of the child support comes from the way we look at the child support payment. If the absent parent, instead of viewing the payment grudgingly, can understand that the child support check represents a statement of care and concern for the child, a faith in the future well-being of the child, and a commitment to see that the child achieves that well-being, then it may be a little less difficult to sign the check each month. If the family receiving the check can see that check as a statement of trust and commitment from the non-present family—an obligation/responsibility with concomitant rights—then perhaps the check can be received a bit more graciously.

A Venue for Ministry

As our friends read through this chapter, the most common response was "all these things will help, but you don't understand how bad my ex-husband (or wife) is. He (or she) has no desire to work things out peacefully."

And that may be true—and it may never get better—but at that point God can open the door for ministry. One hallmark of the mature Christian is a willingness to be used of God in any situation in which he gives us an opportunity to join with him in ministry. I can think of no place more difficult to minister than in the midst of a severed relationship. When we encounter our spouse's ex-husband or ex-wife, when we try to talk about the future of children whom we care about very deeply, when we run into those inevitable conflicts that all parents are going to have—in those moments we can demonstrate that there is something genuinely distinctive about being a Christian.

As I read through the New Testament I am struck again and again at the grace under pressure demonstrated not only by Jesus but also by his apostles. Jesus instructs us in Matthew that he demands mercy, not sacrifice; in other words, he is more concerned about relationships than he is about rules.

In the relationship between the two families, we can forever assert our rights, we can flex our muscles and show our unwillingness to budge or compromise, or we can stand for principle while at the same time showing that we are not just looking out for ourselves or trying to show how tough we are. We can show that Christians are people who refuse to return evil for evil. Instead, we give good for evil, and we minister wherever we find opportunity.

Compassion, openness, concern, and *never* condescension will do more than all the tough courtroom fights in the world for the well-being of our children. Whenever we encounter the other family, God has presented us with an opportunity to model wisdom and love. It must not be wasted.

113

CHAPTER EIGHT

Spiritual Nurture

To bring up a child in the way he should go,
travel that way yourself once in awhile.
—Josh Billings

The story of Moses' early life is a story of divine provision under difficult circumstances. A royal decree had gone out from the pharaoh that all male Hebrew children were to be put to death. The mother of Moses understood a higher calling—the God-given responsibility to see that she met not only her child's physical needs but his spiritual needs as well. The story of Moses is a story of divine protection and provision wrought through the activity and caring of a mother during the most difficult of times.

If, as we discussed in Chapter 6, creation and redemption both involve a divine/human partnership, then, in the care of children, we find that God has called upon parents to participate in both the creation (through birth) and the redemption (through spiritual nurture) of the child. That God allows us such participation must be an indication of the great importance placed upon such a task.

Most Christian families take the biblical injunction to "train up a child in the way he should go and when he is old he will not depart from it" very seriously. We genuinely desire that our children mature not only physically, but also spiritually. Throughout Christendom, however, there is no unanimity of opinion as to what spiritual maturity is or how it is to be accomplished in the lives of children. Therefore, in most Christian homes, the parents' own beliefs and convictions are imprinted upon the child through example and instruction. The parents, not the state or the schools or even the church, are given primary responsibility for the spiritual upbringing of their children.

In a traditional nuclear household, the parents, through both agreement and compromise, together determine how the child will receive religious instruction. Denominational issues, frequency of church attendance, perspectives of the role of scripture in the life of the child, and behavior should be determined, at least at an early age, as the parents strive in concert to provide a healthy Christian atmosphere in which the child can grow wise in the ways of God.

In the stepfamily, the issue can become much more complicated. Ideally, whenever a child's biological parents are no longer married, they both still hold similar Christian values and have similar perspectives on the spiritual health of children. In those instances, it becomes a matter of conversation and reinforcement between the biological parents to ensure that both are kept abreast of the child's development and that both are "on the same page" in trying to meet the child's spiritual needs. We will deal with this preferred situation in the second half of this chapter.

Unfortunately, however, most children of divorce are not so blessed as to have parents working toward the same goal for the spiritual well-being of the children. Instead, they are left with one of two situations. First, and increasingly prevalent, is a situation where one parent is an active, participating Christian and the other is either not a professing Christian or takes no interest in the spiritual well-being of the children. If the Christian parent is the managerial parent, then the Christian parent can easily set the agenda for the child's Christian education, especially at the early stages of the child's development. Most states give the managerial parent the responsibility for religious instruction of the child.

The most difficult aspect of Christian instruction is the situation where one parent is explaining to the child why the church and Christian living are important in the child's home even though they are so unimportant to the absent parent. Such a problem is exacerbated when that parent chooses to denigrate the church and Christianity. Tragically, in some cases the non-Christian parent sees the issue of Christian faith as an opportunity to strike out at an ex-spouse and accuses that person of hypocrisy and self-righteousness.

Though an attempt should be made to discuss with the non-custodial parent the problems that occur when one parent does not support the other in the spiritual nurture of the child, more often than not such discussions are very rough going. No area (including child support) touches a sensitive nerve more quickly than one

116

which portends to confront the eternal destiny of a child's soul. Very little is usually gained in such discussions. Nonetheless, the attempt must be made, but with the recognition that the non-managerial parent may not be amenable to your views.

When there is conflict between a Christian parent and a non-Christian parent, great care must be given to instruct the child carefully in your understanding of what a Christian response is to a nonbeliever—a response of respecting the other person's dignity and right to choose, all the while firmly holding to your Christian convictions. This means that you and your spouse must learn to articulate your faith, and the child must see that faith integrated into your lifestyle; faith cannot be divorced from living. The moment it is, the child will recognize that hypocrisy and very possibly reject a Christian confession in favor of the nonbelief of the other parent.

A more difficult situation arises when the parent with custody is the one who has no interest in the things of God while the non-resident parent feels a great obligation to help the child find Christ and grow in the ways of Christ. We must be honest with ourselves. In four weekend days a month and a few weeks in the summer, it is very difficult to mold a child, to "bring him up in the ways he should go." That means that the very most has to be made out of these times.

Because most states do grant the managerial parent responsibility for religious instruction of the child, if the non-managerial parent intends to discuss Christianity and direct the child toward a relationship with Christ that is not in keeping with the instruction—or lack

117

thereof—that the child receives in the managerial home, you absolutely must first discuss your position with the managerial parent. To refuse to do so could feasibly entail involvement of the courts and result in a curtailment of your involvement in the child's life. Therefore, you and your spouse must be very, very careful in these issues.

At this point Christian wisdom and spiritual insight must play a part. You and your spouse must not get tied up in peripheral issues that detract from the central question of the child's relationship with God. In other words, your spouse's child may not be involved in the denomination of your choice, may not even be as active in church as you would like, and may receive no religious instruction at home. If, however, you and your spouse choose to make those things an issue, you may lose the opportunity to have positive ministry toward the stepchild.

Instead, the focus must be placed on projecting a positive Christian lifestyle at all times. Regular prayer times, family Bible study times, conversations about morality from a biblical perspective, and church attendance should be a part of your life at all times. When your stepchild then comes into your home, he or she is able to see that your Christianity is not peripheral, is not extraneous, but is an integral part of your existence. That experience, coupled with an attractive lifestyle (that is, the child sees that there is not only an experiential difference in the way you live your life but also a qualitative difference—that Christianity does not just speak to eternal destiny but also to who and what we are while we walk this earth), then the child can be drawn as much by your lifestyle as by your words. In such a way, you are not "forcing" your religious beliefs or dictating them to the child. Instead, in the most natural and open setting possible, you are giving the child an opportunity to choose for himself what God desires for everyone.

Remember that you are not in this task alone. At the end of the book of Matthew we have what has come to be called the Great Commission. After Jesus sends out his followers to testify to what he has done in their lives and can do in the lives of others, he concludes with the phrase "and lo, I am with you *always*" (Matt. 28:20).

We have often drawn a word picture from that phrase in which we are sent out on a divine but dangerous assignment with the assurance of divine protection. I do not think that is what is meant there at all. Instead, this is a statement of a royal partnership; Christ invites us to participate with him in the activity he most enjoys: calling others into relationship with him. When applied to our family it means that in all our efforts, God is genuinely excited about the opportunities for our children and stepchildren to come to know him and that he desires to join in a divine/human partnership so that we, with him, can accomplish that task. Therefore, we approach the situation not with trepidation but with eagerness, knowing that we are doing it with God.

Whose Church?

For many of us who were in our youth a generation ago, the community church was a source of stability in our lives. Our world of acquaintances began to expand in the children's program, most of our friendships were developed in children's choir and youth group, and our youth leaders were the adults to whom we felt we could turn in confidence and trust to help us through rocky days.

In many homes today, the church family functions in the same way. For children of divorce and remarriage, the church can be a vital source of stability even while we recognize that, as always, the stepfamily's equation is a little bit more difficult to balance. The child who is away from home every other weekend cannot count on the regular Sunday encounter with other Christian friends and families. Sometimes this means that, on occasion, the stepchild will be put in the awkward situation of explaining the frequent absence, of not being able to participate in certain activities such as a children's or youth choir which involves Sunday afternoon rehearsal time, and of occasionally missing out on some of the really enjoyable experiences simply because of inability to be present.

Whenever possible, the ultimate answer is for the child to be in the same church every Sunday. If both families reside in the same city and there is not a great deal of hostility between the families, it is often very feasible for the families to worship at the same church each week. In that manner, the stepchild can participate fully in all of the activities of the church. That is the ideal.

Unfortunately, it is also the exception. Therefore, the biological parents and stepparents should design a level of church participation that is best for the child. In many cases, this means making sure that if visitation ends on a Sunday afternoon, every Sunday evening the child is in church participating in youth and children's activities and thus "only" misses two Sunday mornings a month. Many families also find that Wednesday mission activities, choir, or youth Bible studies fit the family schedule well. I do know of other families, however, that believe the addition of mid-week activities to a schedule that is already full because of the time the child is away from home puts too much pressure on the family. That is why it is important to seek godly wisdom and insight as to how the family will develop and operate.

Participation in the Watershed Moments

Throughout the life of a child raised in a Christian home and in the church, certain moments assert themselves as being of particular significance to the spiritual and religious life of the child. Professions of faith, baptisms, and recognition and commissioning services can be watershed moments in a child's spiritual journey. It is incumbent that the managerial family extend a very serious effort to include the non-resident parent in these moments as much as possible, even if it sometimes means postponement or rearranging of a schedule.

Most parents, even those who are not particularly religious themselves, nonetheless want to be present for the significant spiritual moments in their child's life. It is a time of bonding between the parent and the child, and it is a major step on the road to fulfilling spiritual maturity. The managerial family's integrity in including the non-managerial family in these moments does more to establish trust and openness in the relationship between the two families than almost anything else. The inclusion of both parents acts as a statement that all concerned really do have the child's best interest in mind and that each family also has faith in the good intentions of the other family as far as the child is concerned. In such manner long-shut doors can be opened.

Modeling Christ

No doubt about it, just as with everything else in the stepfamily's life, the process of spiritual nurturing of the stepchild is much more complicated, and occasionally convoluted, than it is in the traditional nuclear family. But complicated and convoluted do not necessarily mean "worse." In fact, it can be much, much better. If you deal with the difficult issues of religion and your Christian faith with integrity and your life reflects the words that you speak as you consistently model the type of life that you understand Christ to demand from you, your stepchildren have a chance to see the hard side of faith.

In many homes, children are by and large protected from the rather difficult realities that will someday comprise their adult life. Parents are careful that their children do not see the dark side of humanity and that the Christian walk is presented in an upbeat and positive light. Life does not always work that way, and the stepchild understands perhaps better than anyone else that we are not always dealt the hand we want in our lives. The stepchild sees the awkward situations and the difficulty that is intrinsic to the family situation.

If, along with that viewing, the stepchild also sees a consistent modeling of Christ with grace under pressure, an application of the principles of faith not in an abstract manner but to the difficult relationships that are a part of our lives, then the stepchild can understand a truth about this world. He can learn that the walk of faith is a genuine walk, that depending on God is a positive thing, and that the principles of Christian life really do work.

As a stepparent, you and your spouse have an opportunity to present in a living laboratory the reality of Christianity to the children. Though difficult times come along in the life of any family, your Christian faith can rain blessings upon the lives of your stepchildren as God uses you as the vehicle of their redemption.

CHAPTER
NINE

The Weekend
Invasion

Children think not of what is past, nor what
is to come, but enjoy the present time,
which few of us do.

— Jean de la Bruyère

When we talk about stepfamilies, we usually concern ourselves with the stephome in which the child
resides. There, simply because of proximity and time,
most life situations are encountered and the stepparent
has the most active role in the rearing of the children.
When the stepparent, however, is the wife or husband of
the non-managerial parent, the time with the children is
usually limited to two or three weekends a month plus a
specified time in the summer. The nature—and the
nurture—of those weekends varies widely and wildly
from stepfamily to stepfamily. In some, it is described as
a horror without equal; in others, it is a time of joyous
celebration. For some stepfamilies, the weekend visit is
a time of renewal and refreshment, while for others it is

a desperate chance to maintain bonds, correct perceived wrongs, and offer a bit of nurture to the child.

For almost all stepfamilies, however, some difficulty is involved in the biweekly visit of the stepchild. Much of this challenge is rooted in the stepchild's perception of his or her role in the home. The child's perception is usually linked to the reception received from the biological parent.

The greatest mistake most parents make when they are allowed to see their own child only on a part-time basis is that of trying too hard. For example, the father who does not have custody of the children naturally wants to make sure that they understand he is their dad and loves them and is deeply concerned about and committed to their well-being. So the father puts pressure on himself, and concomitantly extensive pressure on the children, to make sure that the relationship is on good terms.

Many non-managerial parents, for example, do not recognize the difference between the child's coming into their home and feeling at home and coming into their home and considering it home. Child psychologists are almost unanimous in pointing out that children need one place to call "home." It gives them a sense of security and a recognition that that is where they belong.

Because many non-managerial parents want to remind the child that they are also the parent and want to make sure the child does not feel deserted, they will refer to the visitation home as the child's "other" home. By so doing, with the very best of intentions, the non-managerial parent is attempting to maintain a semblance of naturalness in the relationship. "I am still your parent,

125

and this is still one of your homes, although you are not here all of the time."

What the parent does not realize, however, is that this is done more for the benefit of the parent than for the child. If the parent is there for the child and makes that home a comfortable place to be, the child will understand the nature of the parent/child relationship. But no matter how comfortable or how accessible the non-managerial parent's home is, the child is not going to consider it home. Home is the place to which the child returns from school. Home is where the child keeps his everyday belongings. Home is where she lives. Try as they might, children are probably not going to perceive the visitation home as the "real" home and may feel a great deal of guilt because they know how much the parent wants them to think of that place as home.

What the non-managerial parent should seek instead is to make the children feel at home rather than consider themselves at home. Whenever possible, children should have a place that is exclusively theirs, whether it is a section of a closet, a drawer, a bed, or an entire room. If they can have a place that belongs to them, while perhaps never considering that place to be their home, they will nonetheless feel at home and have a sense of ownership in the household.

Though not always possible, in some cases it may be a good idea for the non-managerial parent to provide all of the personal belongings that the child needs so that he or she does not have to bring a suitcase for the weekend visit. Clothing, toiletries, games or sporting goods, and a few other necessities and luxuries will make it feel much less a "just visiting" transition. If the non-managerial parent is able to provide a sense of constancy, a sense of permanency, and to ease the transition as much as possible, then this household can become, if not the "other" home, at least a home away from home. And, in such an environment, relationships can be maintained and growth can be experienced.

Your Child, Not Mine

A good friend of mine is married to a man who does not have managerial custody of his children. Instead, his two daughters visit every other weekend and for several weeks in the summer. Because of his job requirements, he is sometimes home only half of the time during the children's visit. The stepmother is left to entertain and care for the children during his absence.

The mother of these young girls has problems of her own. Because of her own insecurities, she has poisoned the girls' minds against their father and especially against their stepmother. Additionally, the children have been taught by example and instruction that striking out in anger is the best method for resolving conflict. When they come to his home, their father, who is a strict disciplinarian, can handle them. They are usually on their best behavior for him, however. When he leaves, the two girls, especially the older one, strike out verbally—and occasionally physically—at their stepmother. Now that the father and stepmother have children of their own in the home, they have genuine concerns about the disruption these visitation periods are causing.

One factor that they and all non-managerial families face is the stepparent's difficulty in establishing a relationship—which we often call bonding—with the stepchildren. If the parents do not put the demands of emotional immediacy on the stepchild/stepparent relationship, the bond can be formed over a period of months—or even years—as the two parties learn to trust, accept, care for, and love each other. The non-resident relationship, however, does not have the convenience of proximity which can allow the relationship to mature. Instead, stepparent and stepchild are called upon to become acquaintances, friends, and then family members through a series of weekend encounters.

The situation is often compounded by the disruption brought into the home by the stepchild. No one's children are perfect, and when a stepchild comes into a home, the faults may become exaggerated in the eyes of the stepparent and resentment may grow. Perhaps he is competing with the stepparent and half-siblings for the time and the attention of the parent; perhaps she is engaging in conflict with the other children there, or maybe either simply feels at home enough to just generally be a child who needs correction. Many stepparents would join in a chorus with the stepmother who said, "I love my stepson; it's just that I can't stand having him here."

Parents naturally take their children's side in disputes, so the parent may feel obligated to stand up for a son or daughter. In a conflict between half-siblings, the stepparent will frequently take up for a biological child. Again, conflict is born, and the already difficult weekend becomes more difficult.

For the parent, this can be a very frustrating enterprise. What father does not want his children to get along with his wife, even if she is not their mother? What mother does not want her children to get along with her husband, even if he is not their father? Watching the non-progress of the stepparent's and stepchild's transition from stranger to family member can be very frustrating. Often, a parent will push and shove, trying to make things work. Instead, the frustration is exacerbated, the problem worsens, and we find ourselves locked into a cycle from which there seems to be no escape.

Entertainment Biweekly

Your husband (or wife) sees his son and daughter only on two weekends a month. So what does he do on those weekends? Naturally, he tries to make the days as good as they can possibly be. For many families, this means that every other weekend the home becomes fantasy land. The usually absent father or mother tries to express love for the children in ways that are emotional, physical, and material.

While the sentiment is good, the effort is often misplaced. Of course, the weekend visitation should be a positive experience for the child. In most cases, however, psychologists tell us that normalcy is the best thing for the child to find. In most households, weekends are a special time. Cartoons take up Saturday morning, and Saturday or Sunday afternoons provide times for family outings. Instead of trying to win the weekend through spending, parents can discover that what the child needs most is time with them and with their stepfamily.

The children, as if they were at home, should have regular responsibilities (such as keeping "their space" clean or helping in the kitchen), should be required to be obedient, and should respect the household rules. If,

129

instead, children are allowed to "get away with murder," are pampered and waited upon, and are showered with gifts, they will have a false sense of reality. They will begin to believe that such should be the norm instead of the exception.

For many children, the return to the managerial home will then become a drudgery almost beyond bearing. They will continually bemoan how "super" it is at the other house where they do not have chores and where Dad or Mom buys them neat things and lets them have sweets all weekend long. They will then live their lives in a fantasy world of wishing that life was always as it is on the special weekends. When the managerial parent and stepparent try to impose the order and reality of a household, the child will rebel and not understand why life cannot always be as good as it is on the visitation weekend.

But is that not a good way to gain a more favorable relationship with the children? Of course, but only if you are willing to sacrifice the present and future well-being of the children for the sake of a positive review. Indulgence spoils children, and spoiled children consistently grow up to be maladjusted adults. Is the parent who regularly indulges his children in order that they prefer his home over the other genuinely seeking the best interest of the children? No, not at all; yet many parents never develop the self-discipline necessary to say no to their children; and their children pay the price.

Therefore, the non-managerial parent must not succumb to the temptation of trying too hard. What a child needs from a parent is not lavish manifestations of affection but consistent caring and integrity. Although financial exertion may require less effort than emotional and physical exertion, what the child needs is time—time with a mother or dad and time to develop a relationship with the stepfamily.

A Spiritual Retreat

A hallmark of Christian spirituality and pietism throughout the ages has been the time of retreat, the time when an individual would attempt to reestablish those values most important to the Christian walk. It strikes me that the visitation weekend can genuinely be a time of spiritual retreat for the child; that is, a time when the child is reminded about the important things in life. Instead of packing the weekend with endless activities and sending the child home exhausted on Sunday night and unable to get enough rest to meet Monday morning's school obligations, perhaps the visitation weekend can be a time when commitment to one another and commitment to important values are imprinted on the child's life. This can be done no matter what the age of the child.

First, the child should not be overwhelmed by the weekend. A consistent diet, consistent time of rest, and a consistency in the emotional interplay among the child, the parent, and the stepfamily are absolutely necessary. Second, the child must have time to just "be a child." Times to play (preferably with a peer), rest, and just be alone are all absolutely essential.

In the time spent with the family, however, the activities provided should vary from week to week. On some weekends, vigorous and more lavish entertainment may be provided (a ball game, a movie, a visit to a theme park). On other weekends, moments of relaxation (a picnic lunch at the lake, a horseback ride, a drive through the countryside to watch the leaves change) can provide a time for parent and child to be alone and talk about the important things in life. Also at those times the child needs just to come and be a part of the family; no special activities, no fuss made, but just interacting in a normal family setting with the stepfamily.

At least periodically, a child needs time alone with the parent. This entails a separation from siblings as well as from all other members of the stepfamily. If, for example, two children come for visitation every other weekend, perhaps once every few months one child can spend Saturday with the stepparent and step-siblings while the other child has a day alone with the parent. In the normal family situation, time alone with each parent is a critical part of the bonding and growing process. For the absent parent, such time is precious and hard to acquire. Therefore, the extra effort required to gain such time is absolutely essential.

The Gracious Return

Still, a difficult aspect of the weekend is sending the child back to the managerial parent, knowing it will be two weeks (or possibly longer) until the next time of visitation. I know of both fathers and mothers who are brought to tears every time they tell their children good-bye. The pain of separation can be very real.

With that pain of separation comes a natural desire to try to manipulate the child's loyalties. Many children are sent back with anger and resentment at the managerial parent that has been engendered by conversations during the weekend. As tempting as it is to try to manipulate the child so he will want to be in the visitation home (even when he is in the managerial home), such action must be avoided at all costs.

If the parent genuinely loves that child, the parent is going to want the child to be as happy as possible in the home where the vast majority of time is spent. Therefore, the weekend should be a time not only of enhancing the relationship between the non-managerial parent and the child but also of encouraging the child and of trying to build a positive image of the home in which the child lives all of the time. To do so shows the maturity of individuals who think not about themselves but who place the child's needs first.

Saying good-bye is tough, but if the visitation weekend becomes a time of recommitment, of enjoyment of the relationship, and of confirming values, then the parent can send the child away knowing that even in absence the parent is still an active participant. And by so helping to carry the load, though in absentia, the parent is fulfilling that divine/human partnership.

CHAPTER
TEN

Strangers
in My House

Children are all foreigners; we treat them as
such.

—Ralph Waldo Emerson

In most families, the time of summer youth camp
is a time of excitement and anticipation. As the day
approaches for the kids to load onto the church or
organizational van, children eagerly greet friends with
whom they will be spending the week, parents bite their
lips with a pang of separation and fear of the unknown,
and counselors attempt to keep from being overwhelmed by the pressing mass of young humanity.

During the week when the children are gone, parents
experience the loneliness of an empty house, happiness
at the opportunity the children have, as well as relief at
the chance for some time alone with their spouse. Parents may also entertain just a few questions concerning
how the child will return to the family. We have all heard
parents remark, "I can't believe the changes in my child

during just the week of summer camp. I hardly knew him when he came home."

If you are a stepparent in a managerial home and the non-resident biological parent has standard visitation rights, you and your spouse may experience the same emotions not just for a week or two in the summer, but probably at least two weekends each month throughout the year and perhaps at least half of the summer months. So many parents watch their children leave, happy that they are getting to spend some needed time with the parent who is not always present, but also with at least some degree of fear and concern. As we said earlier, divorces occur because of conflict, and it is not easy to send a child away with the one whom your spouse may blame for that conflict.

Many stepparents affirm that it is not the child's leaving that is the difficulty, but rather the return. They are not suggesting that it would be better for the child to stay away; indeed, most stepparents I have talked to dislike the whole process of visitation and wish the step-children could stay with them all of the time. Instead, the problem lies in the changes that occur in the child while the child is away from home. Many stepparents talk about the difficult readjustment period the child faces upon returning home. This time is often frustrating not only for the child but also for the parent and stepparent.

Why the Changes?

A few years ago two good friends of mine moved from North Carolina to central Texas. They left family, friends, educational institutions, their church, and jobs and journeyed over a thousand miles to complete doctoral work. They left the mountains and came to the plains. They traded family for strangers. They were removed from a progressive social milieu and found themselves in a very politically and socially conservative environment. They experienced what we call "culture shock."

Their mannerisms and "Eastern" social customs brought smiles to the faces of their new friends in Texas. That did not surprise them. What did surprise them, however, were the constant comments from the folks back home about the changes that their new environment had wrought on them. Throughout the years of their sojourn in Texas, their immersion in a new environment changed mannerisms, speech patterns, and perspectives. For any person actively engaging in a new setting, it could not be otherwise.

In the same manner, we cannot expect our returning children to come home to us "the same." Their time in a new and different environment necessarily produces both short-term changes in personality and long-term changes in character. Our ability to recognize the difference between the two will largely determine our reaction toward the changes and our ability to insulate the child and ensure future well-being.

The word *personality* comes from the word *persona*, which refers to a role that is played or a mask that is assumed. It is that which is temporary—what we place on ourselves in order to control what the world sees in us. Conversely, the word *character* evolved from the time when scribes wrote by pressing a stylus into a soft clay tablet and then waited for the tablet to harden so as to make a permanent indentation in the tablet. Personality is what we present for the world to see; character is what we really are.

As parents and stepparents, we must be much more concerned with our children's character than we are with their personality. Most changes that occur during a short visitation time are changes in personality and must be treated as such. By and large, such changes are no cause for panic; they do not reflect badly upon either parent, nor do they represent an abusive or harmful relationship. Instead, personality changes usually reflect interaction with a changing environment.

Many factors interplay to bring about these changes. As has already been discussed in the chapter on discipline, biological parents often have different and occasionally conflicting expectations of behavior. When a child is immersed for three days or six weeks in an environment in which behavioral expectations differ from "the norm," an emotional reaction will quite naturally take place when the child returns home and is expected to immediately shift the focus back to the previously established standards. That reaction may be one of resentment, anger, or even belligerence.

A second factor that often comes into play has been touched upon throughout the preceding chapters. If a parent is inclined to manipulate the children by criticizing the other parent, the times of brief visitation often provide the necessary interval for doing so. Children naturally question parental authority; they question why, how, and when decisions are made that affect their lives. Many rules, no matter how well thought out or how genuinely important, do not make sense to children.

Additionally, the natural and necessary process of gaining independence involves some level of rebellion against authority; it is part of a child "stretching the wings."

Given this natural inclination of children to question authority, not surprisingly, when one parent has criticized an ex-spouse's parenting style, a child will find in that criticism added justification for questioning authority and rebelling. In one case, a managerial father had decided not to allow his son to participate in a camping trip with some friends but without adult supervision. The father did not believe his son was ready for an unsupervised night in the woods. The young man, genuinely wanting to participate, was very upset with his father.

The boy's mother, seeing an opportunity to score points as the "reasonable" parent, took advantage of a weekend visitation to degrade her ex-spouse, suggesting that "he won't ever let you grow up." In so doing, she reinforced the feeling the boy already had. When he returned to his home, he flew into a rage, berating his father with the same charges the mother had advanced. It was only through excellent self-control and a superb demonstration of parenting skills that the father was able to reach a reasonable and caring agreement with his own son.

We could cite many other causes for the sometimes difficult transition of the child returning home. A common denominator, however, underscores almost all of these factors. In virtually every case, the challenge for the child is related to a sense of frustration he feels as an outgrowth of his questions concerning self-identity and the relationship to parents and stepparents. This frustration is especially pronounced when events and circumstances have placed undue pressure on the child to "choose between parents."

This pressure can be subtle—an offhand comment of slight denigration of one parent—or it can be more open—an attempt to get the child to engage in an activity of which one parent would not approve but the other parent does. Even more overt, some parents put the child in awkward positions by asking questions such as "Don't you love me as much as your mother?" Whenever such pressures are exerted, the child will not easily fit back into the environment. Instead, questions will have to be answered, and the managerial parent will have to exhibit genuine gentleness and patience in helping the child adjust once again to the home.

Reestablishing Order

"Damage control" is an old military term that has found its way into common usage. In both its historic and contemporary meanings, the phrase refers to the process of limiting the scope of injury to an individual or an organization and then restoring that unit to its functional integrity. Damage control is exactly what we must practice when children are returned to us in emotionally volatile states. We must first isolate the situation so that it does not erupt into a major problem, and then we must specifically deal with the issue at hand.

We must recognize the frustration, aggression, or agitation for what it is and not try to place it into the larger context of our relationship with the children. In other words, don't make a mountain out of a molehill.

139

When a child returns home and exhibits symptoms of frustration, more than anything else, the child is crying out for reassurance. Instead of confrontation, this is the time for understanding. A smaller child may need to be taken into your or your spouse's arms so as to feel the reaffirmation of love and affection. The adolescent child may just need to hear, "Remember, we're on your side." An immediate confrontation over "intolerable behavior" will only serve to reinforce the frustration the child already feels. Of course, children must be disciplined. Of course, they must understand what is acceptable behavior and what is not. But the wise parent or stepparent picks the moment. There are times for confrontation, and there are times for reassurance.

As we discussed earlier in this chapter, whenever a child returns home, a time of questioning authority and testing limits is a natural by-product of that return. At that time the parent must gently but with certain firmness reinforce the previously agreed upon standards of the household. The child must not be allowed to discover that he or she can come home making demands, rebelling, and challenging authority with impunity. We do not want to be "quick on the trigger," but neither do we want to excuse the behavior. This is the time that the wisdom of Solomon and the patience of Job must become part of the parent's arsenal. We reassure, but we are firm.

Preventive Medicine

The old adage "an ounce of prevention is worth a pound of cure" is certainly applicable here. If the parent and stepparent can help the child openly discuss and anticipate the challenges inherent in the weekend or the summer time away from the child's residence, the child will be better equipped to handle those situations. Most children cannot immediately tell you why they are acting as they are. They do not recognize their own frustration, resentment, or insecurity. Instead, they ascribe their aggression or unacceptable behavior to origins that have little to do with the true source of the problems. A first step in resolving behavioral problems is to discover the genesis of the difficulty. Then, steps can be taken to address the source of the problem and thereby find a viable solution.

Younger children are especially susceptible to questions of security. When a young child experiences divorce, in the child's mind there is a concomitant experience of desertion. When Daddy leaves, he's not just leaving Mommy; he is also walking out on the child. Explanations and protests to the contrary never quite resolve the problem of desertion for the child. When that child is "sent away" for a weekend or for the summer, the child quite naturally perceives that separation also as a type of desertion. The child is going to need some help dealing with those feelings.

If potential feelings and questions are addressed before a child leaves for a weekend or a summer vacation away from home, the child will be much more likely to recognize the feelings for what they are when they arise. That early recognition will often help the child resolve the problem on his own. Or, at least, the parents will be able to get to the source of the problem more quickly and thereby seek resolution. This is especially true in questions of security. If the child is helped to understand that it is natural to have questions about where he fits in the family order and about the security of relationships and is reassured beforehand that his position in the family is certain, he will be much more able to deal with those questions when they arise.

Divine Insulation

The task of parenting begins, is permeated, and ends with prayer. No place is this more true than in the stepfamily. As the apostle John neared the end of his long ministry, he came to view the members of his ecclesiastical flock as his children. He had a great care and concern that they be protected from the wiles of the world. Though Peter warns that "the devil walks about like a roaring lion, seeking whom he may devour" (1 Peter 5:8), John reassures us, "You are of God, little children, and have overcome them, because He who is in you is greater than he who is in the world" (1 John 4:4). The promise of God to us and our children is never a promise to remove us from a path beset with evil. Rather, the promise of God is that he will go before and protect us in the midst of evil.

Give the gift of prayer to your children. Before they leave for their time away, even as they eagerly anticipate an enjoyable time with an absent parent, help them to understand that in both the good and the bad times God walks with them, loving, protecting, and nurturing. Pray for them, and pray with them. Let them know that you ask God to divinely insulate them from the challenges that are too much for them to overcome on their own— that you ask God to be an active participant in their lives.

Creative Time with Your Spouse

It is little wonder that most programs of positive

thinking have their roots in, or at least a loose connection to, the tenets of Christian faith. This is because the gospel of Jesus Christ, the Christian life, and the doctrine of divine activity are the ultimate statement of positive thinking. Whenever a Christian encounters difficult times, the question must always be asked, "How can God use this situation to bless me?" The first few verses of Matthew 5 take very difficult situations—to be poor in spirit, to be meek, to be persecuted—and call all of those situations "blessed" because of divine activity in them. Romans 8:28, while by no means suggesting (as some people seem to think) that everything is always as good as it possibly could be, does promise that no matter how difficult the situation, God can use the circumstances to bring benefit to our lives.

Many couples in stepfamilies have had the most difficulty for their marriages during those times when the children are absent from the home—and at any given time, the children are away from 50 percent of all stepfamilies. Most parents, no matter how good their relationship with their ex-spouse, both miss the children and are concerned about their well-being. Additionally, the parent is unsure about the "proper" level of contact during the periods the children are away and often has many questions about how the child will return. Is it any wonder that these times put a great strain on marriages?

In these darkest times, however, God can take the pain and turn it into opportunity; the bane into blessing, the grief into growth. But, as in creation/redemption, God relies on the human/divine partnership of collaboration to accomplish the task. God can use you not only to minister to a concerned parent, but also to strengthen significantly the depth and breadth of your marriage.

Most parents find that a great difficulty in their marriage is the lack of private time together. All couples require such times for communication, for sharing of thoughts and concerns, for bonding, and for affection. Especially in the younger household, such quality private time is very difficult to come by. In the stepfamily, however, such time is usually built in. The semi-monthly and summer visitation times can provide a needed respite for the parents in the stepfamily.

The wise and creative stepparent is the one who recognizes the difficulty of the transition from the full house to the empty house and vice versa, but he or she is also the person who recognizes the absolute necessity of developing time as a couple together. In a marriage where no children are present, the couple has a transition time during which they can get to know each other more closely, understand each other's character and emotions, and begin to find their method of living together.

In the stepfamily, however, the couple is not awarded that luxury. Instead, it is *family*—parents, children, house, dog—from day one. Therefore, the couple should continue the process of growth together as a couple by regular intervals of time alone. While it must be recognized that the pain will not evaporate nor will the concern disappear, God's ministry to your spouse through your activity can make the difficult time a time of renewal.

CHAPTER ELEVEN

But I Want to Be Called Dad!

Speaking personally, I have found the happiness of parenthood greater than any other that I have experienced.
—Bertrand Russell

There are times when parenthood seems nothing but feeding the mouth that bites you.
—Peter De Vries

In Michael Crichton's science fiction thriller *Jurassic Park,* a group of geneticists in the not-too-distant future find a way to clone dinosaurs from DNA salvaged from fossilized remains. Their attempts to capitalize on their genetic research go catastrophically awry, however, when they discover that their creations are more intelligent, more aggressive, and more agile than they had ever imagined. The carnivorous reptiles turn their island paradise into a Jurassic meat market as they prey on everything that moves. The geneticists find that their best laid plans and safeguards are woefully inadequate, and their attempts to do something positive and profitable have led to disaster. Things just do not turn out as they had planned.

On a much more personal level, those of us who are stepparents usually discover that things have not turned out exactly as we planned. The very fact that you have picked up this book and are reading through it indicates that you most likely entered into a marriage relationship with every intention of being an active participant in your stepchildren's lives. If you are like most concerned stepparents, you really did not anticipate a stepfamily but rather a nuclear family in which you just happen not to be the biological parent of the children. It might have only taken hours, but almost certainly did not take much longer than a few days or weeks, before you discovered that life in the stepfamily and as a stepparent is not the same as life in the traditional family with children and two biological parents.

To be sure, many of the great assets and privileges of family are available to the stepfamily. Loving bonds can be developed; laughs and stories can be shared; heartbreaks and fears can be soothed; and both parent and stepparent can have adventuresome, loving, affirming relationships with the children in the household.

At the same time, however, if the stepparent and parent entered the relationship with the expectation that the reconstituted family would be no different from the nuclear family, then they almost certainly were disappointed by the outcome of their efforts. The stepparent usually sees himself or herself as a full participant in the rites of family.

Often, however, the stepparent is expected to fulfill the duties of parenthood and yet is denied many of the

privileges thereof, often even the privilege of being called
Mom or Dad. Do the challenges intrinsic to the stepfamily
invalidate the relationship? No, for what many stepparents
discover is that, if the stepparent understands the dynamic
of the relationship between stepparent and stepchild, that
role can be the foundation of a deeply meaningful and very
fulfilling relationship for the stepparent. No, you are not
Mom or Dad, but you are an integral part of a child's life,
and you and your stepchild can both have a richer existence because of your presence.

Identity Crisis

Mother. Father. Mom. Dad. Mommy. Daddy.
Stepmother? Stepfather? The titles that designate familial relationships fill a significant percentage of
Webster's New World Dictionary. Most children grow naturally and easily into the less formal titles for their parents.
The titles often change through the years from Ma-ma
to Mommy to Mom; from Da-Da to Daddy to Dad, perhaps to Pop. All reflect the special relationship and
bond between parent and child.

A real challenge in the stephome is deciding what the
new stepparent will be called. Many non-resident parents stridently protest any parental affirmation that the
child may give to the stepparent, thinking the stepparent
has encroached upon the parent's "territory."

At the same time, "Stepfather" or "Stepmom" is a title,
not a name. No one would feel comfortable being called
that. Should the child then call the stepparent "Aunt"
or "Uncle" or by a first name? That, somehow, seems a
little too casual—not really providing a description of the
relationship that exists. If the stepmother has come in

and taken care of the household, helped provide income for the family, wiped a little girl's tears, cooked, washed clothes, and bathed the children, does she not only deserve the title "Mother" but also the name "Mom"? In many stepfamilies, such confusion leads to an identity crisis of the first order.

We can make no universal statement about this issue. For some families, the new stepparent will be called Mom or Dad. For others, it may be a first name. For still others, a special form of affection may develop—perhaps a nickname that connotes the relationship or one that recognizes a special affection.

Most important, however, is helping children to understand that it is not in the name but in the relationship that the real life of the bond between stepparent and stepchild exists. We need to teach our stepchildren that the critical factor is not what we call someone who enters our life but how we feel about them and how we relate with them. Ultimately, this is a lesson that not only our children must learn but that we must learn ourselves.

The Stepparent Who Wants More

Much of the challenge inherent in the stepfamily situation finds its genesis in our refusal to recognize the difference between parents and stepparents. In some families where the stepparent entered the children's lives when they were very young and where a biological parent is permanently out of the picture, these differences are minimal. The children may view the stepfather as their father, may call him such, and may relate to him as such. In many stepfamily situations, however, both biological parents play an important role in the lives of their children. That is as it should be. Children should never have to feel that they have been deserted by a parent. Children should know their heritage and should grow to maturity under the care and instruction of both parents.

Sometimes, however, the presence of both biological parents in a child's life makes the stepparent feel like the odd man or woman out. The stepparent then has a very difficult time seeing what role is to be played in the child's life. "She already has two parents, so what am I?"

In most stepfamily situations, the non-managerial parent, though still active in the child's life, is not there for the day-to-day care and upbringing of the child. Therefore, the stepparent is left to fulfill all of the roles and duties of "parent" and yet often receives little or none of the perquisites that go with the job. As one stepfather expressed it, "I am the one who is always there for them. I bring home the paycheck. I put a roof over their heads. I stay up late at night when they are sick. I make sure they get to the ball game. When they need to be disciplined, I'm a part of it. I am everything anyone could ask a father to be to my stepchildren.

"Why is it, then, that I always have to be second in their lives? My children are much more concerned with what their dad thinks about their grades, their friends, and their behavior than they are about what I think. I never see my kids on Father's Day. And no matter what I do or how often I'm there for them, I know that my stepson's ultimate loyalty will always be to his dad. I know that my stepdaughter's father will be the one to walk her down the aisle at her wedding. I guess I somehow thought that over time he would disappear and I would become the father. But it just hasn't worked out that way."

The same lament is heard from stepparents everywhere. It seems that this difficulty is based in expectations. Though most stepparents would say that they went into the marriage with their eyes wide open, few genuinely understood what to expect. Therefore, in the midst of the marriage, the stepparent is called upon to make an honest reevaluation and redetermination of that role.

Such an analysis must not focus on the negative. If we really get down to brass tacks, parents of all varieties— biological, step, foster, adoptive—feel unappreciated and taken for granted. Such is the nature of the role. Indeed, if called upon during their children's teenage years to evaluate what it means to be a parent, even biological parents in the nuclear family might quickly decide that the tribulations of parenthood far outweighed the triumphs.

Especially in the stepfamily, while we do recognize the difficulties, we must be ever cognizant that the stepparent/stepchild relationship can be a divine provision for a broken family in a fallen world. In Frank Capra's Christmas classic *It's a Wonderful Life,* Jimmy Stewart plays a man who, contemplating suicide, is given the opportunity to see what life would be like if he were absent. As he walks the streets of his neighborhood and sees the broken families and dreams that were never fulfilled simply because he was not there, he realizes the great value of his contribution.

As a stepparent, you may not be called Mom or Dad, but that in no way diminishes the value of your contribution to your family. Abstract yourself for a moment if you can from the reality in which you live, and picture your family without you. Picture a little boy who does not have someone present every day to throw a ball with him. Picture a little girl who never learns the fundamentals of cooking because she sees her mom only occasionally and then there is really not enough time. See, if you can, a man or a woman faced with the prospect of raising a family alone. See your spouse without a shoulder to lean on, without someone with whom to share the fears and joys, the tragedies and the triumphs.

Contributions that you make are critical not only for the well-being of the family but for the stability of our churches, our country, and our world. Studies have consistently demonstrated that children raised in a two-parent home (be it with both biological parents or in a parent/stepparent situation) are better at school, are more dutiful citizens, and are much more likely to grow up to be productive members of the community. Your stepchildren need you, and they need your presence.

It seems the problem for most concerned and caring stepparents is that they really want to be the parent; that *stepparent* simply is not good enough. Why? *Because stepparent is a negative term.* The stepparent is not seen as someone who can enter into a loving relationship with the family. The stepparent is not seen as someone who contributes to family life. The stepparent is seen as a poor substitute for the real thing, an adult present only because of a relationship with the child's parent, a disciplinarian who may view the child as an unwelcome encumbrance at best or free labor at worst. The life of the stepchild is depicted as a cold, lonely existence—a child with one parent missing and the other monopolized by someone who does not want the child around.

Even our literature and language are replete with

defamations of the stepfamily. The Cinderella step-mother syndrome finds its way into print much more often than does the stepparent who is a vital member of the family. To be treated like a stepchild is to be rele-gated to second rank. It is little wonder that we all want to be more than "just a stepparent."

With nearly half of all American children living in a stepfamily situation, it is time that we who are in the stephome begin to speak very clearly about the role of the stepparent. No, we are not biological parents. Our chil-dren may not call us Mom or Dad. We may not be accorded many of the accolades that comprise the parent's life. Nonetheless, we provide nurture—physical, spiritual, and emotional. We are there for the child in the child's time of need. We are at the school play, often in the back-ground, but nonetheless there. The stepparent is not the interloper but the one who stepped in to fill the role that someone else (for whatever reason) chose not to fill.

The stepparent, and those associated with the stephome, thereby have an obligation not to allow "step-parent" or "stepchild" to be a term of disgrace but rather a badge of honor. We are the ones who have taken on the often thankless task of raising someone else's children. We are the ones who give ourselves openly and freely, recog-nizing that there are limitations to what we will receive in return. Our society needs to understand that we are step-parents not because we could not have children of our own or because we got stuck with second best, but because we chose to enter a stepfamily relationship.

Then What Am I?

If, then, the stepparent is neither parent nor an

untoward appendage to the family, then what is its definition? A stepparent is a stepparent—a role that may be more than a parent and less than a family member, occasionally both at the same time. Ideally, the stepparent is someone who has joined in a partnership with God, with a new spouse, with stepchildren, and even, hopefully, with the other biological parent. That partnership must provide a loving, caring home within the context of a divinely ordained and blessed marriage in which children will grow to become committed and caring Christian adults.

Children of divorce already have a strike against them. For whatever reason, they have seen a parent leave. In all likelihood, they have seen acrimony and anger between their parents. They have found their home to be, rather than a place of safe haven and nurture, a place of tension that offered no respite from the pressures of the world. Into this environment walks the stepparent. Perhaps initially perceived as the intruder, the one who put the final nail in the coffin of Mom and Dad's marriage, the stepparent stands in a unique position to both love and nurture as well as receive love and nurture from the newly budding relationships.

In forming these relationships, the stepparent can help a stepchild to understand that the stepchild is valuable and worthy of love. No matter how hard the biological parents work to help children understand that the parents, not the children, were the cause of divorce and that they are not unlovable if a parent leaves because the marriage is breaking up, most children of divorce still carry feelings of inadequacy and guilt. When the stepparent enters the child's life, the forming of a loving and caring relationship between stepparent and child can salve those wounded hearts. The child is worthy of love. The child is capable of relationship. The child is "good enough" that someone chose to come live with her.

Such healing only occurs, however, when the child sees herself as a full participant in the formation of the new family. She must not feel that the stepparent/stepchild relationship was "dumped on her." Instead, the child must feel that she had a choice also. Although it is helpful, it is not absolutely necessary that the choice be made before the wedding ceremony. Instead, the child sees choice as participation in the development of the new relationship.

This means that the stepparent must not come on like a gangbuster. We earlier discussed the myth of instant love, and many stepparents expect to walk in and receive full-fledged membership in the family from the beginning. Instead, give the child time to learn to trust, love, and respect you as your relationship grows. The demand of immediate affection casts love in a bad light. Then, instead of seeing herself as a worthy participant in a love relationship, freely receiving and returning affection, the child more likely will see love as an artificial act that has little to do with heartfelt concern and affection.

Through daily contact with your affection and your concern, the child can come to perceive himself or herself as someone others really want to get to know, as someone who causes relationships to be formed rather than ended, and as someone capable of loving and being loved. With a self-perception so grounded, a foundation is prepared for the child not only to be an emotionally healthy member of the family during childhood and adolescence, but also a lifelong contributor to the family during adulthood when forming lifelong relationships of her own.

Modeling a New Type of Parent

The stepparent, as she or he interacts with husband or wife and even with the other biological parent, can also demonstrate to the child that conflict and disagreement can be resolved in a civil and Christian manner. Psychologists tell us that children of divorce have very poor conflict resolution skills. The lack of ability to deal adequately with disagreements almost certainly arises because the children have seen their parents model the wrong way to settle disputes.

Indeed, a very significant portion of divorces occurs because husbands and wives have somehow discovered that shouting and inflexibility are the operative methodologies for marriage. When children see such behavior modeled on a consistent basis, it is little surprise that these children grow up and have marital problems of their own. They have never learned how to do it differently. The stepfamily must, therefore, learn to resolve disputes in a civil and Christian manner—and the parents must set that agenda. The children need to learn that shouting does not facilitate the settling of disagreements. Instead, it causes small disagreements to inflate into large ones.

Children must learn that the heart of relationship is compromise, meeting someone halfway so that all opinions and positions can be treated with respect. If a child can see the parent and stepparent model a style of resolving conflicts through affirmation of one another

155

in love while recognizing the other person's right to an opinion, then the child will be provided with the tools to incorporate conflict resolution skills into his or her own life.

Ultimately, to be a stepparent is to be a role model. The only question is over what kind of role model we will be. The actions we take, the attitudes we exhibit, and the agendas we set will all teach our children about what we think is important in life.

Our children may never acknowledge the lessons they learn; indeed, they may not *realize* they have learned anything at all. Nonetheless, you can affect their character in a way that will last throughout their lifetime. One of the most striking passages in Scripture comes when Paul, calling himself the Corinthians' spiritual father, encourages them to "imitate me" (1 Cor. 4:16). Can you say that to your stepchildren? Can you tell them, "Do it the way I do it"? Can you suggest to them that your lifestyle will be sufficient for them? You have an opportunity to model. What are you doing with it?

And God Will Bless

One of the most important truths in Christian life is often overlooked: We are seldom blessed by those we bless. More times than not, God does not choose to reward our faithfulness in serving others by having those we serve return the same graciousness toward us. Far too often we hear stories of a good deed done which was unnoticed and unappreciated. While we should never excuse that kind of behavior, perhaps God allows it to be that way so that we do not serve others simply for what we get out of it.

Instead, when we are faithful in service yet do not see an immediate return, God promises blessings—be it the blessing of his activity in our lives or the blessing of his people's activity in our lives. More often than not, we probably do not see the cause-and-effect relationship, but we do have a genuine awareness of God's presence and his care and concern for us.

So goes it also with the tasks of stepparenting. Oh, the "thank you's" are nice, the "I love you's" are genuinely appreciated, and the little girl's smile can make a stepdad's day, but that must not be the ultimate answer for us. We do the things we do as stepparents because we see the hand of God in our lives—the hand of God calling us to ministry as surely as any pastor stands in the pulpit.

To be certain, we must not enter into a stepfamily relationship with a rescue mentality—the "I'm going to make it better for everyone" syndrome. But at the same time, we recognize, as we have entered this love relationship with a new husband or wife and their children, that we are called to perform a divine service.

Just as surely as a mom or a dad or a pastor or a missionary receives a divine commission, so also are we called to be a part of the outworking of God's divine plan. We fulfill all of the tasks of parenthood. We thank God for the opportunity to participate. We do what we do not for the accolades but because we love God and our families.

CHAPTER TWELVE

The Family Beyond

I'm not sure I like this. I've just got too many relatives now.
—A first grader, meeting his
stepfather's family for the first time

Mothers-in-law get a lot of bad press. The 1950s popular recording "Mother-in-Law" bemoaned the lot of a couple whose marriage was torpedoed by the wife's interfering mother. The husband idealizes the marriage without her interference and cries out, "Why can't she just leave us alone?" And so it goes—in advice columns, television shows, and literature—not just the mother-in-law but all the extended family are often presented as the foremost obstacle to a happy and stable marriage.

Especially for the stepfamily, which is called upon not only to balance in-law relationships but also to factor in relationships with the ex-spouse and that family, it often seems that it really would be easier just to get away from everybody, to sever all relationships and start all over. Ultimately, however, the extended family relationships can be a source of stability, encouragement, and joy for those in the stepfamily. They can provide both the fresh perspective and the constancy of support and love so vital to the healthy home. Such positive results, however, are realized only when all parties involved commit to overcoming the obstacles to relationship and to expend the effort necessary to make those relationships fruitful.

What are the dynamics of the relationship between stepfamilies and the larger family, especially grandparents, aunts, and uncles? Each person involved in these relationships needs to know how their actions affect the situation. We must realize that each person in this extended family brings his or her own set of values and ideals and his or her own perspective and personality. Therefore, all of the extended family must be entered into the equation of our discussion.

Accepting the Possibility

Most parents eagerly—with only a little trepidation—look forward to the time when a son or daughter calls home or drops by and says, "I've been seeing someone I'd really like you to meet." The realization that a child may be on the verge of a lifelong marital relationship also marks a passage in the parent/child relationship. It is a time of excitement and a new beginning. Along with that excitement comes concern for the health and the direction of the new relationship. In most cases, the family can somehow participate in the courtship. To some extent, the growing family relationship parallels the dating relationship, evolving from acquaintanceship to affection to a firm commitment of love.

Despite the "forsaking all others" of our marriage

vows, the extended family remains a part of the marriage relationship. Marriage and family counselors often know that marriages have a much greater chance of success when the extended family—parents, brothers and sisters, grandparents—of each spouse have made a love commitment not only to their biological family member but also to the new spouse. Such a commitment calls for enlarging our emotional tent, welcoming a new person into the family circle, and willingness to see things from a new and fresh perspective. That "there's someone I want you to meet" certainly changes things.

Indeed, the whole context changes more than just a little when the aforementioned announcement is followed by the explanation, "Yes, she has been married before." Such a pronouncement is certain to bring some very hard and pressing questions from concerned family members. Add to that the statement, "and she has a wonderful little girl," and you had better be prepared for some very serious discussions.

For the family who had always assumed that a beloved child would meet someone (preferably at church) from a similar background and that the commonality of that relationship would blossom into romance and then into a burgeoning love and finally marriage and family, the discovery that the son or daughter is dating someone not only with "a history" but also with a child is quite a load to handle. Parents want their children to have successful marriages. Parents are not fools; they know the divorce statistics. They understand—both from personal experience and from observation—just how tough marriage really is. They also know that a person who has already experienced a divorce is even more likely to be a candidate for a second divorce. Therefore, concern for their child is inevitable.

It is not all that much easier for the family that hears, "I'm getting married—again." They have already seen a son or a daughter live through one divorce. Perhaps even more telling, they may have seen a grandchild view battling parents or the recriminations of a nasty custody trial. They are not prepared for themselves, their child, or their grandchild to go through that again.

The family witnessing such a turn of events most certainly has many questions related to the wisdom of a second—or third or fourth—marriage. For one thing, they may recognize much more clearly than the divorced relative that their child was as guilty as the ex-spouse in contributing to the failure of the marriage. They may wonder whether the character traits that destabilized the first marriage have been corrected.

Very often, too, an individual who has been divorced will quickly move into a second relationship. At that junction, parents and family are prone to ask, "Why so quickly? Is this not just a case of rebound?"

They may also have questions about a grandchild's ability to make a quick emotional turnaround. After seeing parents "fall out of love" and the relationship between the parents grow into recrimination, is the child, then, to be expected to shift gears immediately and welcome with open arms a new person in his or her life? We talk about a child's resiliency, but what are the long-term effects of such an emotional roller coaster ride?

These are all valid, legitimate issues for all the families involved in these situations. Sometimes these problems are talked about only out of earshot of the principals, and sometimes they are suppressed, but almost always the questions are present. At the very least, they represent the family's attempt to organize and systematize an overload of new information into some kind of logical order. The questions are a necessary milepost on the road to integrating the new relationship into the larger family.

A Measured Response

The response to the questions is as important as the questions themselves. Notice I use the term *response* rather than the term *answer*. For some of these questions, there is no good answer, but there is always a response.

If the couple is not yet married, they owe not only the family but also themselves and their relationship the time and the effort to evaluate seriously those concerns that have been voiced. Often our family and friends see us for who we are even more clearly than we do ourselves. Our strengths and our foibles are open to their perceptive eyes. If they have serious doubts or serious questions about the timing, then we certainly had better hear their concerns.

The engaged couple should do everything in their power not necessarily to persuade, but at least to patiently answer the questions that have been raised by both families. They should reassure the families that the decisions are well thought out—and those decisions must be well thought out, or they will prove disastrous. More important than the verbal answers will be the physical response given to the family. This response is marked by consistent behavior in all the situations of life. If both families can see that the couple approaches life's challenges with godly wisdom, with patience, with love and commitment, this behavior will go further to answer those questions than any words ever spoken.

A most difficult task that any individual or couple faces is honest self-evaluation. When questions have been voiced by friends and family members, pride makes a genuine and honest introspection even more difficult. The bottom line is that we do not want to admit that our family is right about our weaknesses. But, when not only our future but the long-term well-being of a potential spouse and child or stepchild is on the line, we had better swallow our pride and take the long, hard look.

A walk down the aisle does not resolve all of the questions. The nagging doubts and uncertainties may persist for some time, but do not be frustrated by their persistence. Instead, recognize again that these questions grow out of familial love and concern. Especially when the previous marriage was long-lasting and, on the surface, appeared to be solid and well-founded, a month or two—or even a year or two—of consistent behavior in the new marriage is not going to erase all of those doubts.

Instead, the questions begin to ease when year after year your spouse's family sees you integrate yourself into the family and act in love not only toward your spouse and your stepchildren but also toward your in-laws and their families. Trust is cumulative—slowly. Respect is to be earned through the years. As your spouse's family sees you constantly interacting with your stepchildren, your husband or wife, and with them, they will eventually grow to understand that you are committed and that you are the kind of person after whom their grandchildren can model their lives.

An aside to the extended family: give your children and their new or future spouse the benefit of the doubt. As you know from personal experience, beginning any marriage is very difficult. That difficulty is compounded when there is a child (or children) in the picture. If you have been a supportive and involved family, you have every right to voice your concern and ask the difficult questions. But it is imperative that those questions be framed in a constructive manner. An indictment of your child's judgment and common sense benefits no one. Rather it polarizes and destroys the possibility for dialogue.

When the decision is made and the couple has embarked upon their journey of marriage, those questions should end and support begin. Even if the marriage was not your idea of a good choice, if you are genuinely interested in the well-being of your child and grandchildren, you will do everything in your power to make that marriage a success. That means that you must carefully pick the times to offer words of encouragement—and make sure the words are encouraging, not just an opportunity to get in little shots—and the times to mind your own business. Always ask yourself the question, "Am I doing what I'm doing because I am certain it will benefit all of the relationships, or am I doing it out of less pure motives?" If you can honestly and openly answer that question, then you can be a genuine positive influence on a couple trying to establish a home and family.

Old Loyalties and New Bonds

One woman put it quite bluntly: "I told my daughter that if she went through with her divorce, she could leave and my son-in-law could stay as part of our family. When the divorce was finalized and he was no longer around, I genuinely felt that one of my children had been taken away from me." One of the great tragedies of divorce is that when the separation of a husband and wife is completed, many other relationships—some of which have been forged over a period of many years—are also severed. Regardless of fault or contribution to the ending of the marriage, in contemporary society, divorce almost always means not only a breakup for the husband and wife but also the ending of relationships with their families.

For some families, this can be quite painful because, although the person may be absented from family gatherings, the memories and the loyalties have not disappeared. In many ways, it is like a death in the family. A divorce does not necessarily mean that all of the love has been cut off.

The new husband or wife then walks into this situation. The transition from new acquaintance to family member is always a difficult one, and it is by no means eased when the ghost of a former husband or wife still stalks the family gatherings. As the new addition to the family, you may feel that you are being constantly measured against the previous spouse. Such a feeling can cause a sense of distance between you and your new extended family.

As we have discussed in other chapters, your spouse's family has to make a difficult adjustment concerning the relationship between you and your stepchildren. It may be very difficult for grandparents, aunts, uncles, and older cousins to see the emerging parent/child relationship. They may rightly feel that they have a prior claim on the relationship with the children. They may, therefore, feel a bit of discomfort or even jealousy when they see one of your stepchildren come to you with a skinned knee or a hurt feeling.

When the question is discipline, the problem may be even more pronounced. A grandfather simply may not be able to accept this virtual stranger who has known his grandchildren only a year or two disciplining them in his home. An aunt or an uncle may make a quick judgment that the new stepparent has too quick and too firm a hand in matters of discipline.

Such feelings are usually a natural outgrowth of the protective instinct that God has given us for our families. Indeed, all of the dynamics of relationships discussed in these last few paragraphs are dynamics based in proper and worthwhile feelings of love and loyalty. Although it may be hard to see at this time, these are exactly the types of emotions that you want your new in-laws to feel because they hold a promise that, given time, your extended family can hold the same type of love, esteem, and loyalty for you.

A Response in Time

How then do you respond? Ideally, though difficult, you respond to your new extended family in the same way that you would respond to anyone who expresses care, love, and concern for your family, because that is precisely what is happening. Therefore, you do not get hostile, you don't "stand up for your rights," you don't "let everyone know that you're in charge now." Instead, in the same way we discussed earlier in this chapter, you demonstrate to your new family a lifestyle of care, concern, and consistency, and you let them come to accept you for who and what you are.

Is confrontation—"dealing with the issue"—the best option? That depends largely on the case and the individual. In some families, a good heart-to-heart talk about feelings and concerns is the best way to deal with a problem like this. In other families, you are best just to give it time and let the family learn you as you learn them.

The important thing is not to force yourself on the family. Give them time and space to understand who you are. Under no circumstance should you enter into a competition with the memory of the ex-spouse. Attempting to build yourself up at his or her expense is certainly the wrong path to take. In most cases, as the one who has walked into the middle of these relationships, you probably do not need to say anything at all about the former spouse. If your spouse wants to have that type of discussion with family members, that is one thing; for you to do so carries the appearance of pettiness and insecurity.

Instead, let them find out for themselves what kind of person you are. Showing them your lifestyle will do more to bring you acceptance into the family than any verbal argument you will ever advance on your own behalf.

The Hardest Choices

Unfortunately, even among those of us who call ourselves followers of Christ, some families simply will not accept a son's or a daughter's choice of mate. For reasons perhaps only they can understand, a mother and father or brother and sister choose not to bring a new person into their circle of family. This probably happens more often with the stepfamily than when the marriage is a first marriage for both parties. Possibly because the family may not want to accept someone with a marital "history" and a child or because the family has never forgiven their own family member for the breakup of the marriage, the initial acceptance is more difficult. Unfortunately, such rejections occur more often than we would like to believe.

How do we respond to outright rejection? I believe two principles must be kept in mind in such a situation. First, a husband's or wife's primary and ultimate relationship is to his or her own immediate family: spouse and children. This relationship must supersede all other familial relationships. If parents or brothers or sisters force a man or a woman to choose between families, the choice is clear. A man or woman must always place the relationships of the family which they have formed above all other relationships. The biblical injunction "for this reason a man shall leave his mother . . ." is well taken.

Second, and also very important, you should do everything in your power to keep the lines of communication with the extended family open. Even if there is rejection and an attempt to sever those relationships from one end, we cannot wash our hands of the relationship and simply walk away. Instead, gently and without pushing, we must let our family members know that no matter what their actions toward us, we still count them as family and want to relate to them as such.

Growing into Family

Intrinsic to the definition of the family are the bonds that are formed through years of relationship. Hopefully, we never stop growing in our relationships and our understanding of family members. As my parents grew through middle age into late adulthood, we had many conversations that revealed sides of them I had never seen before. My appreciation for them and my understanding of them continue to evolve as I pass young adulthood and move toward middle age. There is a sense that, as we have all grown older, we are even more "family" now than we have ever been before. I guess you could even say that there are levels of being family.

Likewise, as you seek to be integrated into the larger extended family, at certain levels you will gain acceptance into relationships. Just as in a courtship, your new family will come to know you and gain affection and, hopefully, make that final commitment to you. But, also just as in a courtship, the death knell of the relationship is the pressure of rushing acceptance. You have a lifetime to grow into that relationship.

A demand that you immediately supplant the one who filled this role before you is a demand you must not put on yourself. If you do, you will certainly pressure the new relationships in ways that will retard their growth and prevent them from reaching some degree of maturity. Instead, just as you must do with your spouse and with your stepchildren, allow those relationships to grow and mature—and give yourself the time to become family.

CHAPTER THIRTEEN

The Stepfamily and the Community of Faith

> But go and learn what this means: "I desire mercy and not sacrifice." For I did not come to call the righteous, but sinners, to repentance.
>
> —Matthew 9:13

The institutions of America often advance a societal agenda for the family whose pace and direction cause Christians more than just a little discomfort. We are very concerned—indeed, we are outraged—when we see school superintendents present alternative family settings that include two "parents" of the same sex to elementary age students. We object greatly to sex education classes in which abstinence is never even presented as an alternative. When we turn on the television, we are dismayed to find that promiscuity, marital infidelity, and moral deviance are presented as the standard rather than aberrations.

Unfortunately, however, at the same time, the church

170

has been extremely slow to address the reality of the family in America. Specifically, though with many very significant exceptions, contemporary churches are not prepared to make adequate provision for the stepfamilies who comprise a very significant percentage of the American family. Programs, language, practices, and policies all seem to operate within a framework that not only considers the two-parent, traditional family the norm, but also sees the stepfamily as an exception. The burden is then placed on the members of the stepfamily to make the necessary arrangements so that they can function within the boundaries imposed by the institutional church. For many stepfamilies, this remains an ongoing battle.

The Language of the Church—What Is Family?

We rely heavily on our churches to preserve the traditions, the values, and the rituals that form our heritage. Such reliance is both good and worthwhile. We recognize that the preservation of these values maintains a vital link to the truths of our past. Without that affirmation of tradition, we may lose something of ourselves and be unable to anchor our vision of the future in the deep and fertile soil of our history. Therefore, remembrance and constancy are vital ingredients of our identity.

Unfortunately, many of our churches and church leaders are unable to distinguish between preservation of our history and resistance to change. Very often, a church begins to equate entrenchment with faithfulness to the gospel. Such a refusal to recognize the changing face of present reality confronting us each day is devastating to the church that wants to be a true force of ministry in the late twentieth century. It is one thing to sing about the "faith of our fathers"; it is quite another to pine for those days when the basic tenets of faith and morality seemed commonly acceptable to all those with whom we came in contact, and in such longing, to impose nineteenth-century precepts on a twentieth-century reality.

Too often, the leadership of the institutional church seems to feel that abandoning traditional language (even if that language does not adequately deal with the issues of today) wreaks of compromise, and that compromise is the death knell of morality. As long as the family is strictly drawn with a father in the role of leadership, a subservient mother/homemaker, and two or more obedient children, the black and white answers are easy to give. As such, we are not called upon to make tough judgments. We are not called upon to live within the tension of uncertainty. Such refusal to deal with the reality of what families are today is a form of escapism, an escapism that debilitates the ministry of the church and devastates those families left outside its circle of ministry.

This deficiency is evident in the language of the church. Family, it seems, is very strictly defined. And if the family does not fit into the traditional mold, then the teachings, programs, and focus of the church simply do not apply.

Many churches recognize this tension, but most have had only limited success in addressing the difficulty. "Family" still refers to the traditional two-biological-parent nuclear family. If a seminar on family life is presented, it is almost always from that perspective, and generally not intended for the nontraditional family.

As we have mentioned, programs are presented that take into account nontraditional families—stepfamilies, blended families, single-parent families. But, almost exclusively, these programs are presented from a perspective that sees such family situations as the break from the norm, the aberration. While these unconventional family settings do have special problems and must address issues in a manner different from the traditional family, these families are also just as much a part of the work and life of the church as are the families where two biological parents are present.

If, you may ask, stepfamilies and other nontraditional families have their own set of problems and their own realities, why not treat them as the exception and provide a special (if separate) ministry to them? Is there not a need to focus a special ministry on a special group? Why not do it that way?

The answer is that separation for the purpose of special ministry always also means a lack of integration into the full ministry and program of the church. The stepfamily becomes a special case instead of a full participant.

In the same manner, many awards and recognitions that are proffered to reward children for active participation are based on consistency of attendance. Again, the child with divorced parents is precluded from receiving such rewards or recognition simply because it is impossible to be present every week.

But is not this the price we must pay as part of living with the reality? No, it must not be because the tragedy here is that, for many children who are stepchildren or victims of broken homes, integration into full franchise in the church never occurs. The church never becomes part of the definition of their lives. Instead, church is something they do when they can. These children then grow into adults for whom ministry through the church is but a peripheral concern. Such a tragic loss must not occur for these children—or for the church.

As we move into a new millennium, the church faces competition for the lives of youth as never before. To dismiss immediately almost half of the population through mismanagement of our resources of time and programming is as irresponsible as it is foolhardy. We cannot lose our families—by anyone's definition— through recalcitrant refusal to minister in ways that are unfamiliar to us.

The Ministry: To Be Family

Recognizing the problem, what then is the church to do? We start by changing our definition. As long as "family" refers only to the traditional family, then any request that the church expand the focus of ministry to include those families not constructed along traditional lines will be a special pleading and thereby perceived as a self-pitying cry for special treatment. The "exceptional" ministry, then, will be seen as an accommodation for those less fit, and, again, the stepfamily will not be integrated into the full fellowship of the church.

Instead, the definition of "family" must include the diversity—and the richness—of what it means to be family in the church today. The easy answer is that families ought to be composed of children living with their biological parents. The reality, however, is that within the walls of our churches there are about as many children from nontraditional families as there are from traditional.

But when we change the definition, doesn't that mean that we give our stamp of approval to this type of living situation? Yes, it does, of course! But that is the point. This is not a statement that the single-parent family is preferred or that the stepfamily is the best living arrangement. No one would make that claim. By affirmation of the stepfamily, the message is not that this is the biblically preferred family structure.

We affirm, however, that the stepfamily is a viable institution, an institution that can be used of God to meet needs through ministry. We also instruct the members of our fellowship that we cannot isolate ourselves from the reality of our society. No, divorce is not the right answer. No, divorce is not the best choice. But when we encounter those who have been victimized by divorce—through their own choice or through the choices of others—we nonetheless have an obligation to join with them in a partnership of ministry, a recognition that God can use us for the good of his kingdom wherever we are in our lives.

Ultimately, family must mean family. By whatever name the family is designated—be it traditional, step, or single-parent—it has an obligation before God to live righteously, to teach the children morality, and finally, to be an active part of the ministry of a local congregation. A segregation, intentional or not, resulting from a mind-set that sees only the traditional family as the "real" family prevents Christians from participating in the full ministry of the church—from doing what Scripture commands them to do. And such prevention is precisely what Paul is talking about when he admonishes us never to be "stumbling blocks" (Rom. 14:13).

As the church gains a full understanding of what it means to be family, it is then called upon to be inclusive in its programming. Whenever possible, the church should go the extra mile to ensure that activities are scheduled not only for fullest participation, but in timeframes that are the least exclusive. To do so, both the stepfamily and the traditional family must recognize a full partnership in the ministry and program of the church and be prepared to compromise for the well-being of all involved. For example, in the children's choir situation, it very well may be that the majority, for whom Sunday afternoons are most convenient, need to sacrifice their convenience to provide at least a possibility for the minority to participate.

In a like manner, scheduled events such as youth retreats probably need to take place on a Friday night and Saturday or not at all. For many stepfamilies, scheduling then becomes very difficult. The stepfamily cannot expect the church to schedule around "our child." Instead, the stepfamily has to recognize that the program of the church must go on, and the stepfamily can either find a way to accommodate by switching weekends and rearranging schedules, or the court-ordered reality will simply have to win out.

Compromise and recognition of the rights and needs of others are required on all sides in such a ministry situation. At times, the traditional families must go the extra mile to accommodate the needs of the whole

176

church, while at other times the stepfamily will be called upon to make the sacrifice. All the while, all members of the body must strive for a ministry and cohesiveness that draws the fellowship of believers together.

The Body of Christ

The Pauline epistles are ripe with illustrative metaphors that paint a portrait of the Christian faith and life. Particularly because the church was a new entity, Paul was especially conscious of using word pictures in his writings to help the young congregations firmly apprehend what it means to be the church of Christ.

One of the most telling metaphors he employs is that of the body. By calling the church the body of Christ, Paul implies that it is a functional, integrated entity. Each part of the body must fully participate in the work of the body if life is to be sustained. Different body parts fulfill different functions, but all are vital to the ultimate success of the composite whole. Some parts or organs may be less noticeable or receive less attention, but they are nonetheless vital to the success—indeed the survival—of the rest of the body.

In a like manner, we who comprise the church are different in our self-identity and in our gifts. For the church to be a successful, functioning entity, however, each disparate member must be drawn into the full circle of ministry. For its own sake and for the sake of all the different types of families that comprise it, the church cannot afford to retreat into a fortress mentality that excludes those who do not fit a pre-cut pattern.

Perhaps the most ringing challenge to Christian faith occurred when Jesus commissioned Peter and established his church. Jesus promised ultimate victory for the church, stating that "the gates of Hades shall not prevail against it" (Matt. 16:18). Too often, our exegesis of this passage leaves us with an understanding that Jesus portrayed the church as a great fortress that offered protection from the world. If we look closely at the words, however, we can see very quickly that such a perspective is not at all what was intended in the passage. The church is clearly portrayed, not on the defensive, but as the agent of attack moving forward and breaking down the barriers to freedom and righteousness that surround us everywhere.

Too often, unfortunately, we do have a fortress mentality in the church. We want to huddle behind the cloistered walls and long for the days when there were fewer challenges to the integrity of our Christian walk. Ultimately, however, such an understanding of the church is certainly not biblical. We are to be marching out, confronting the world, recognizing the reality in which we live, and seeking to call all to righteousness.

The front lines in such an offensive must be our families, because it is family members in the workplace, in the community, and in the schools, who immediately encounter the world. Therefore, the church's call before God is to integrate and incorporate all families—regardless of their designation as traditional, step, or single-parent—into full fellowship and ministry.

CHAPTER FOURTEEN

No Child
in the Middle

A thick skin is a gift from God.
—Konrad Adenaur

Scripture records the poignant story of the two women coming before King Solomon, both claiming to be the rightful mother of the same child (1 Kings 3:16-28). Confronted with their competing claims, Solomon offered a solution: The baby would be cut in half and one half given to each woman. The baby's real mother, of course, could not bear the thought of her child being so destroyed; therefore, she immediately insisted that the other woman be given custody of the child. Solomon, recognizing the maternal love and knowing that the child's true mother would always ultimately put the child's best interest above her own, gave custody of the child to the woman who was unwilling to see the child slain. The moral: True parental love would never sacrifice a child for self-serving ends.

If only today's parents—especially divorced parents—could comprehend the reality of that truth. Instead, children are consistently manipulated to meet the ego needs of parents engaged in battles of superiority with each other. The most common complaint that children lodge against their divorced parents is that one parent uses them as a weapon to punish the other.

To a surprising extent, the stability of the stepfamily rests on the biological parents' willingness and ability to accept their divorce and the court-decreed living arrangements without constantly using the children as pawns in an internecine warfare. When the relationship between the two families is rocky, when the children are constantly called upon to choose which family they "like" best, when they constantly hear one parent belittle the other parent, the turgid relationship is a threat to the very stability of the family.

Conversely, if the parents can find a way to work together and choose not to act out their insecurity by attacking each other through the children, the relationship can become a positive building block by providing a context of love and support for the children. The children are able to move easily back and forth between the two families while learning that disagreements can be handled in a forthright and fair manner. The way that children in stepfamily situations see the adult members of their extended family interact with each other will to a large extent determine how those children learn to deal with relationships in their lives.

Your Problem, Not Your Child's

Although the eighties gave rise to the "me generation," the dysfunction known as egocentrism is far too extensive and pervasive to be limited to one decade. We live in a self-indulgent world and a hedonistic society. Moral restraint and self-control seem to be increasingly rare, and the stepfamily is not exempt from its effect. The "putting the other parent down through the kids" syndrome is precisely about self-indulgence and immaturity.

Two impulses seem to be behind the desire to attack the other parent through the children. First, a divorced spouse may find that the children are convenient messengers through which to get in a few cheap barbs at a former spouse. Most parents find it particularly grating to be themselves attacked by others in front of their children, so the wounds left by such maliciousness can be particularly painful.

Second, the most prevalent cause of such attacks may be a natural and probably unavoidable competition between any divorced couple for the affection of their children. Parents want their children not only to love them but also to think that they are "the best." Such is the nature of parenthood. When a divorce has occurred, the competition level between parents increases.

The divorced individual not only seeks the merit or approval of his or her children but also finds in that approval confirmation of the validity of his or her own self-worth. Part of that image comes from the affirmation of being the "wronged" party in the divorce; that is, no matter who initiated divorce proceedings, the divorced individual wants to feel that he or she was the "right" one in the marriage, through the divorce, and in the present situation.

Therefore, a parent will often seek the children's approval by regularly attacking the children's other biological parent. In so doing, every time a child agrees with the criticism level, that parent has "scored points" in the ongoing battle. And the children function as pawns in the individual's battle for self-esteem.

Parents engage in the petty battle of ego stroking in the midst of protestation that they are looking out for the best interest of the child. Nothing could be farther from the truth. Genuine concern for our children would mean that we would never stoop to draw them into the vortex of a storm between two parents. Instead, we would do all we could to build up their image of their parents. We would focus on positive qualities rather than negative attributes. We would give the child the healthy self-confidence that comes from the full assurance that both parents are worthwhile, quality individuals of integrity.

The message that all parents need to hear is this: It's your problem, not your child's. As Jesus demanded of us: "I desire mercy and not sacrifice" (Matt 9:13). With that statement, he placed a demand upon our lives that, instead of focusing on how well others are keeping the law and doing what we think they should, we seek to live in harmonious and peaceful relations with them. We forgive first and ask questions second. By so doing—refusing to use our children as couriers of malicious intent—we become a force for peace and a pillar upon which our children's future can rest.

Refusing to Play the Game

Parental ire is raised quickly when a child responds to a query concerning misbehavior with a "he started it." In most households, we hold the respondent as equally at fault with the one who initiated the whole proceeding.

The same rule needs to apply to parents. If we are to have a successful, communicative household and somehow manage to maintain a relationship with the other biological parent of our stepchildren, then we must find a way to deal with this whole issue of one-upmanship. The two hard and fast rules are (1) Don't start it and (2) Don't participate in it once somebody else has started it.

Refusing to return evil for evil, and instead insisting on returning good for evil, is an end worthy in itself. But this issue goes beyond that. This really is a matter of protecting our children. Because it is an opposite standard from the one the world embraces, we must demonstrate to our children again and again that problems and disagreements are never resolved by returning what we receive. If we choose to drop into petty name-calling and character attacks as a response to the barbs directed at our own person, then we have absolutely failed in communicating to our children the most basic lesson of Christian character.

But won't our children perceive non-responsiveness to personal attacks as a sign of weakness? Aren't we being "pushed around"? Yes, if all they see is non-responsiveness from you. That is why we return to the principle we learned in Chapter 2. Genuine meekness is strength, power under control or restraint. In other words, we must let our children see that our non-responsiveness is a choice—not because we are cowering in fear, but rather because we are strong enough not to respond in kind. Instead, we respond always seeking to be redemptive for ourselves, for our children, and for the other family.

How can that be accomplished? Initially, this demands open lines of communication with our children. We do not sit and silently steam when we are told of malicious words directed at us. Instead, we talk openly and honestly about why those things may have been said. We constantly seek to develop with our children an atmosphere of trust. We let them see constancy in our words, our motives, and our deeds. Then when attacks are leveled against us and we openly address them, our children can trust what we say and the reasons we say it, and give us the benefit of the doubt whenever they hear attacks upon our person.

We must also learn to measure and control our response. When our children come home with an honest question about an issue that has been raised concerning our parenting style, our provision for them, or choices we have made—and we explode at the very thought that someone could question what we have done—they will learn very quickly that some subjects are off limits. Items of conflict will become items of non-discussion.

Yet, no matter how sharp the barb, how deep the cut, how unjust the charge or how malicious its intent, we must respond reasonably. It does not hurt to show anger, but it cannot be an anger that frightens the children. They cannot be afraid that we are going to "pick up the phone and have it out right now." Instead, they need to see that we will respond with measured care and genuine concern.

Finally, we must make certain that we do not allow our discussions with the children to become an opportunity to get in our own shots—and that is oh so tempting. When we do that, we respond in kind, not returning good for evil. We communicate to our children that everyone should look out for themselves and that Christian behavior extends only to certain arenas of our lives. No, even when we respond to the attacks, a Christian demeanor must be present, and a desire for ministering to our family and those who cross our path must remain foremost in our minds.

Confrontation

At times the distortions of half-truths and untruths risk such damage to our children and our relationship with them that a response is required. Of necessity, we must confront. We must do so in full recognition that the very act of confrontation may be difficult for us and for our children.

We should carefully pick the time when we have determined that a response is necessary. It should not be in the yard right after the children have been brought home or during a quick conversation on the telephone. If at all possible, a discussion to confront continual abuses by one parent should be a time when both parents (and stepparents, if needed) sit down to discuss a range of issues.

Questions about the way one parent belittles the other should be incorporated into the overall context of providing for the child's well-being. There is absolutely nothing wrong with one parent explaining to the other parent the injustice and general unfairness of such an attack—though such protests will likely have little effect on the offending parent. The focus, however, must be on the damage that is done to the children when they hear one parent accuse the other in such manner.

Confront non-confrontationally. In other words,

don't walk into one of these sessions looking for a fight. This is not a time to bring up old wounds, to rehash old disagreements, or to address past injustices. Deal only with the issues at hand and seek resolution of those issues so that they do not become longstanding problems.

Even if the other party refuses to do so, you must always "fight fair." Do not allow the session to degenerate into accusations and cross accusations. If such a ploy is initiated, don't rise to the bait. Do not allow the discussion to become a trading of character attacks. That is not the purpose. Instead, focus on making provision for a child who does not need Mom and Dad to be at each other's throats. Find a way to make this time redemptive.

Insulating the Child

There are times, however, when the best of intentions and the sincerest of efforts do not resolve the problem. The other parent still, at every opportunity, seeks superiority with the children by putting down the ex-spouse. In such cases, you call it what it is—and let the children see it for what it is. Explain to the children precisely what is going on: they are being used to get shots in as a part of a dispute or attack that was not their making. Do everything in your power to help the children understand that although Mom or Dad might be doing it just that way, it is not the best way—or even an acceptable way—of resolving differences between people. You limit the damage.

This again becomes a time when the children need to see consistency, integrity, and honesty from you and your spouse. Then, they will have less grounds to believe charges against you and more grounds to trust in the things you do for them.

Children are usually smarter and have more insight than the level for which we give them credit. They understand a lot more about the dynamics of human relationships than we realize. More often than not, they recognize petty attacks for precisely what they are. If we give them no reason to doubt us, and instead give them every reason to trust our word, the little shots that may be taken will have only a minimal effect. They need to understand the game and why you don't play.

Finally, never ever forget prayer. The time you spend on your knees both with the children and for the children is time that God honors and returns to us in the form of blessing. We must all constantly pray for our children, especially when they are caught in the vise of a parent who thinks the child is a convenient vehicle for salving old wounds. There is only one genuine insulation for our children, and that is the protection God provides. That insulation comes with absolute non-judgmentalism on the character of the persons involved but with a focus instead upon the act rather than the actor.

CHAPTER FIFTEEN

The Court of Last Resort

In law, nothing is certain but the expense.
—Samuel Butler

This is the chapter of this book that should not have to be written. It certainly seems that someway, somehow, parents—even those who have survived the most hostile and bitter of divorces—should be able to find a way to provide an environment to settle disputes involving their children without involving the judicial system. However, throughout our country, divorced families turn to the courts to seek redress for damages done and answers to conflicts they simply seem unable to resolve on their own.

Ultimately, only a very few of these disputes have any business in the courts. Most of the disagreements that make their way into the judicial system could easily be settled by a pastor, legal counsel, or family therapist. Instead, a father and a mother choose to "have it out" in front of the judge, dragging their family's history, their ongoing relationships, and their children through the mire of a public dispute. Such actions have less to do with justice and concern for the well-being of the family than they do with stubbornness and petty immaturity.

When Should the Courts Enter the Picture?

At what time is it appropriate to seek redress through the legal system? When we speak of settling differences in the courtroom, we are not talking about "paperwork agreements" in which both sides have agreed on a change in child support, visitation rights, or some other matter of management of the children, requiring only that legal documents be filed in the courtroom. Instead, we are referring to those times in which a genuine dispute between the parents leads one parent to take legal action against the other.

It is actually much easier to say when legal action is *not* appropriate rather than when it is. Except in the most egregious situations, the courts are not there to redress a situation in which you think your rights have been violated. Some parents seem to think that any petty offense directed at them is ample ground for a return visit to the judge so that he or she may chastise and correct the offending party. Neither should the court be used as a battleground to rehash the initial court order or agreement unless situations have changed to such an extent that the agreement is absolutely unworkable. For the most part, if you could live with the agreement when it was first made, you can live with it now. Except in rare cases, the agreement should not be changed unless both parents are willing to make the alterations.

In other words, don't go running to the court unless the situation is extremely serious. We must recognize that anytime a child sees his or her parents in a dispute of the magnitude that requires the court's involvement, the child is going to be damaged. For many children, their parents' day in court is nothing less than a rehashing of the fights of the initial divorce. Few children can imagine anything worse.

The courts are an arena of last resort, preserved for that time when the damage being done to our children or our relationship with them outweighs the damage that will be done by a confrontation in court. It is an arena in which serious disputes are to be settled. When we go to court, we must fully recognize that the court battle will take its toll on our children and on their relationship with at least one of their parents. It may forever redefine the way the two parents relate to each other. It may erect barriers to communication that even the most sincere efforts will not overcome. We must, therefore, always ask the question: Is this worth the damage that it will do to the kids?

There are times when the answer must be yes—times when the injury being done to our children or to our relationship with them is of such magnitude that it requires we take a stand. The courts, then, offer us the only answer.

For many Christians, such a decision must be weighed not only against potential damage to the children but also against scriptural injunctions concerning suits and legal action against other persons. Can a Christian, in good conscience, ever turn to the court in a suit against another person?

From a biblical standpoint, I believe an affirmative answer can be justified on two levels. First, the biblical injunctions against lawsuits seem to be specifically aimed at those who are seeking financial redress from another Christian. The Bible is clear that Christians should *not* spuriously enter into such suits. Seeking protection for the rights and the material needs of children is a completely different issue—one for which Scripture lays down no prohibition.

Second, laws are made because of human fallenness. God was the first lawgiver, establishing standards of behavior to protect our relationship with him and with each other. The courts, as the instrument by which laws are fairly administered, are the proper resource to which the Christian can turn for protection. That is why they exist. If the time comes when a parent has no other course but to turn to the courts, that parent should not feel restrained by a Pauline injunction against use of the courts. It simply does not apply here.

Mediation Rather Than Litigation

The inability to find common ground, to find a place for discussion, is at the root of many divorces. A husband and a wife are simply unable to bridge the chasm that separates them. Therefore, communication breaks down and a divorce ultimately results.

Very rarely is their ability to communicate improved following the breakup of the marriage. Instead, it often happens that, unrestrained by the bounds of civility necessarily imposed by the proximity of living together in the same household, what communication exists moves beyond the bounds of common decency and respect of another person. Even when the children are

191

the only topic of discussion, the parents find little common ground at times on which to meet and make accord.

Before the parents turn to the court to settle their differences, they should be encouraged to seek an outside party to mediate the dispute. Perhaps a former pastor or a family counselor can be brought in to offer an outside perspective. Both parents might find that mediation offers a very positive alternative for them. Certainly, parents would like to make decisions about custody, child support, visitation, and resolution of disagreements without having that decision made for them by a third party, which is precisely what happens when a judge is brought into the process. Mediation allows parents to participate more fully in the decision-making process and gives them a fuller and freer sense of control of their own decisions.

Mediation, be it from a formal legal intervention or simply a qualified third party agreeing to intercede, is not to be confused with family therapy or counseling. Instead, this is a chance for two individuals to work out problems between themselves and find the best answers for their children. It recognizes your genuine desire to reach a satisfactory conclusion to a disagreement and affirms a common commitment to the well-being of the children that is shared by the disputing parties. Such a commitment is of immeasurably greater benefit to the children than is the parent so intent upon protecting his or her rights and guaranteeing the well-being of the children that he or she rushes to court at the slightest affront.

CHAPTER
SIXTEEN

Don't Make the Same Mistake: Teaching the Children About Sex and Marriage

Unless the LORD builds the house,/They labor in vain who build it.
                    —Psalm 127:1

When it comes to achievement, stepchildren by and large reflect national norms. They are just as likely to be successful in life as are children raised in traditional families. Both Abraham Lincoln and George Washington were stepchildren. Alex Haley was raised in a stephome. Studies conducted at university campuses, in metropolitan areas, and among larger population groups find that as stepchildren become adults, they are no different from the rest of the population in self-sufficiency, stability, career achievements, or financial success.

In one area, however, children of divorce do not live

up to national expectations. There is a growing realization that children of divorce, whether or not they move into a stepfamily environment, end up with a greater incidence of divorce and remarriage in their own lives. This should by no means surprise us. Children learn more from example than they ever do from lecture.

It is, therefore, especially difficult to teach children of divorce that God intends a lifelong monogamous relationship for husband and wife. That lesson may be especially difficult to convey since divorce may appear to be the easiest option during difficult times. So the Christian parent and stepparent must find a way to help the child gain a positive picture of marriage and a strong biblical foundation for male and female relationships within the context of the Christian home.

Children in the divorced home find it particularly difficult to grasp what God really intends for them in terms of sexual relationship and marriage. Not only do they have to deal with the siren song of society, which says, "Sex between consenting adults (read 'adults' to mean anyone who is old enough to understand the mechanics of sex) should not be affected by moral constraints." Our children are constantly bombarded with that message from their friends, popular media, and society at large.

Even more telling, however, is the fact that the very concept of a single-spouse, lifelong-monogamous relationship has, to some extent, been illegitimized because their parents could not maintain a lifetime physical and emotional commitment to each other. It is very difficult to tell a child, "Save yourself for your husband or wife" when that child perceives, in all likelihood, that there may be two, three, or four husbands and wives during a lifetime. What, then, is so special about saving yourself for a wedding night?

The Mores of America

The sexual revolution of the sixties and seventies did not touch the vast majority of America. You may have heard of "free sex" on television, but unless you lived in Haight-Ashbury, you did not see much of it in your neighborhood. The reverberations of the sexual revolution, however, have permeated virtually every aspect of our society. They are felt in our neighborhoods, our schools, and our churches. Our children live in a world radically different from the one in which we were raised. Elementary school students are called upon to deal with questions of morality that many of us did not face even in high school.

Not only have the pressures of society changed, but physical pressures exact new demands on our children. Since the turn of the century, nutrition and health practices have lowered the average age of sexual maturity by some three months per decade. In our parents' generation, a boy or a girl might not have had to deal with the fires of adolescent hormones until age fourteen or fifteen. Now, the average age of the onset of menstruation in girls is less than twelve years.

While our children are becoming capable of sexual activities at earlier and earlier ages, the typical age for first marriages is getting later and later—up to twenty-five (from twenty-one in the 1950s). Thus, we need to be very aware that when we teach our children to remain chaste until marriage, we are probably asking them to be

195

sexually inactive for over a decade of their life. We are requesting that they do this at a time when they are emotionally immature and, therefore, have great difficulty saying no to peer pressure, physical needs, and emotional "strokes." And their drive for sexual satisfaction, especially in young boys, will be almost at its peak. How many of us would be willing to place the same kind of constraints upon our own activities?

Two decades of sexual permissiveness have reaped a harvest that is a medical tragedy, a social nightmare, and a moral disaster. During the late eighties and early nineties, America was polarized by debate over condom handouts, alternative lifestyles, sex education, and an entertainment industry that encouraged us all to "just do it." Anyone who suggested that restraint and abstinence were the best methods to address the sexual pandemic were dismissed as religious fundamentalists who had little contact with the real world.

As America was shaken by outbreaks of sexually transmitted disease in the eighties, culminating in the AIDS epidemic, questions of morality for many people became secondary to protecting sexually active teens against disease. We were told, "Give adolescents the information to make a wise and informed choice; teach them how to protect themselves. Worry about moral instruction at another time." Sex education was seen as a health issue rather than a discussion of values. If teens are physically capable of engaging in sex, this line of thought proclaims, then they are capable of making their own choices if they have been provided with adequate information.

Although some educators and government officials

have been slow to recognize it, a consensus is growing that such a method of sex education is not reaping the intended harvest. The age of initial sexual activity continues to drop. A 1993 Time-CNN poll found that more than a third of fifteen-year-old boys have been sexually active, as have 27 percent of fifteen-year-old girls. Among teenage girls who consider themselves sexually active, 61 percent have had more than one partner. One teenager reflected the confusion that this approach to sex education has caused: "They tell me to be responsible, but does that mean I wait until I'm married, I wait until I'm in love, or that I just make sure I wear a condom?"

What Does the Bible Say?

Unfortunately, most studies seem to indicate that children raised in Christian homes are only marginally more sexually restrained than the teenage population at large. That means that if we are attempting to communicate a biblically based sexual morality, either our children are not getting the message or it is being drowned out by the decibels of the message squawked out by society as a whole. Perhaps when we encourage our children to "just say no," it rings hollow because we ourselves do not understand the importance of remaining sexually celibate outside marriage. Our Christian theology of sex and marriage has been woefully inadequate.

The Christian understanding of sex and marriage begins with the theology of creation and extends all the way to the doctrine of the church. It permeates everything that we are about as God's people. As we have discussed, when God granted humankind the ability to procreate, it was a statement of his desire to form a divine partnership with us—a partnership in which we would join with him, not only in bringing new life into the world, but in maintaining that life and seeing it grow to maturity. Because creation is an act of love and enjoyment for God, he made it an act of love and enjoyment for us. As we become partners with God when we create, so we become partners with our spouse. Indeed, the bonding and the partnership that is formed are so important that we find divine endorsement of sexual relations between husband and wife even when it is not specifically intended to bring new life into the world. It is not only an act of creation; it is an act of growing love and of growing the relationship.

But the biblical edict goes beyond initial creation because it also gives parents the responsibility to "raise up" children in the ways of God. It demands that the man and woman who have created life have a responsibility to see that life grow to maturity and to provide a context in which the child can fulfill divine intent for his or her life.

In the book of Ephesians, the apostle Paul gives specific instructions about marriage and explicitly tells us that lifelong, monogamous relationships are God's intent for husbands and wives, specifically because God has given the family to us in order to teach us about our relationship with him. The sexual relationship between a man and a woman is sacrosanct; that is, it is not to be violated. Paul instructs us that a man should have one wife and is to be faithful to that wife in order that his children can learn the meaning of fidelity and faithfulness not only to another person, but also to God.

The Christian is to remain sexually pure and be reserved for the husband/wife relationship not only for the societal benefits, but also because that fidelity teaches us about preservation of the church for Christ. As the wife is committed and purely devoted to her husband, so the church holds herself exclusively for a relationship with Christ. When we can catch just a glimpse of the place that God has given the sexual and marital relationship, then perhaps we can begin to communicate the importance of premarital chastity, the necessity of fidelity within the marriage union, and the sanctity of preservation of the marriage itself.

Preserving the Home of Tomorrow

For many teenagers, however, a theological basis will not be the grounds for choice. Perhaps a little understanding of what premarital chastity would accomplish for them might be more persuasive. In the big picture, if one generation were to practice strict monogamy, the epidemic of sexually transmitted diseases would be wiped off the face of this earth. There would be no more deaths from AIDS. While that simply is not going to happen, the individual, nonetheless, can make certain that he or she will not become another statistic. Purity in relationship is simply the ultimate way to accomplish that goal.

Beyond the physical benefits, when sexual relationship is a bond shared only between husband and wife, the couple has avoided the accumulation of a lot of baggage. When the ghosts of old lovers are not hanging

199

around, when one spouse feels that the relationship they have formed was important enough that the other waited for it, when our children can look at their children and say, "I remained pure, and so can you," the benefits to that relationship are immeasurable.

When a relationship, instead, has to overcome past infidelities or when there are hanging questions of future faithfulness, the relationship can never be as secure as when the husband and wife know that they upheld their sexual purity only for one another. Although it may be hard for a fourteen- or fifteen-year-old to catch a glimpse of the benefits of waiting, through open communication and an open relationship with them we can help them to understand that chastity is the ultimate choice for those not in a marriage relationship.

Do As I Say, Not As I Have Done

Ideally, every Christian should say as Paul does: "Imitate me" (1 Cor. 4:16). Unfortunately, in the stephome, the child may find very hollow and hypocritical our insistence on proclaiming the sanctity of a monogamous relationship in which the boy or girl awaits marriage before engaging in sex. The child can rightly charge the parent, "You've had more than one partner, so what makes preserving my virginity until I am married so important?" Until you and your spouse are ready to deal with that question, you cannot hope to promote an environment in which your stepchild can legitimately measure the worth of your pronouncements about the sanctity of marriage.

Only when we are willing to acknowledge that divorce is wrong and not what God intended do we have a voice that can be heard by the teenager growing up in today's world. In a society where divorce is seen as a quick and easy solution to a marital spat or boredom with the same sexual partner, or as a way to escape responsibilities, children raised in stephomes need to see their parents take responsibility for their choices. They need to understand that parents recognize that divorce, under almost any circumstance, is an evil—albeit at times a necessary one.

The child's own experience of divorce can be drawn into this discussion. Even when the stepfamily life has been a positive one for the child, when there has been a great relationship with the stepparent and/or stepsiblings, the child needs to understand that, ideally, God intended one man, one woman, and their children to live together until those children reached the age at which they would form their own families—and that way is still best.

Perhaps at the point of discussion of sex, marriage, and relationships, you and your husband or wife can talk to the child about some of the difficulties that are borne specifically because of divorce. Talk about the complications in relationship. Point out to the child the times in his or her life when having a stepfamily simply was not as good as having a traditional family. Your openness and honesty will perhaps help the child to make a commitment to a purity in relationship and will be the buoying float that carries the child's future marriage relationship through troubled waters.

To be sure, a child must understand (as we explained in Chapter 1) that God makes provision even for fallenness. A few years ago, I counseled a teenage girl—a freshman in high school—who, because of insecurity and a searching for love, had started having sexual relations with a twenty-one-year-old man. As that relationship ended and she was faced with the results of the choices she had made, I heard her say, "If there could only be some way I could become a virgin again."

Unfortunately, she could not, and many teenagers who find themselves in a similar situation decide that since the "damage has already been done," a promiscuous lifestyle is an acceptable alternative. The negative self-image that developed because they engaged in sexual intercourse (which they understood to be wrong) becomes a self-fulfilling prophecy as they become more and more sexually active.

It is at just that time that they need to hear a word of God's grace from us. Do not allow them to forget that our God is a redeeming God. Remember the words of Jesus to the woman who was caught in adultery? "Neither then do I condemn you." Christ did not want her carrying the baggage of her past mistakes, but he did not leave it at that. His next words were, "Go your way and sin no more." It is not enough to say that, when we seek his forgiveness, God is not going to hold against us the things that marked our lives in the past. We must help our children to understand that God still has positive expectations for their future; God wants them, even if they have fallen, even if they have made bad choices, to be restored and to live lives of purity and holiness.

A Covenant of Positive Sexuality

Sex is more than just plumbing. Too often our approach to sex education, whether in the school, the church, or the Christian home, is reduced to a mechanical explanation of genitalia and how intercourse works. At the same time, however, we in the church have carried inhibitions about sexuality that may have been just as dangerous as the permissive attitudes of society.

A man relates the story of how his father, a well-educated Christian, conducted his "sex talk" when the man was a boy of thirteen. "He took me out to the farm and pointed out the parts of the male and female. Then he explained to me how a bull mounted a cow. I asked, 'What about people?' He responded, 'We don't talk about people.'" End of conversation. No affirmation of the goodness or the rightness of sexual expression. No recognition of the divine gift of the bonding between husband and wife. No statement that God's provision is also pleasurable.

As Christian parents begin to talk to their preteens and teenagers about sexuality and sexual expression, there is a tendency either to make sex "dirty" and reduce it to plumbing, or conversely, to spiritualize sex and talk only about the depth of experience and feeling. Teenagers will be quickly put off by either approach. Instead, a covenant for sexual purity that can be made with teenagers is an affirmation of the goodness of sex and also a recognition that such bonding is very pleasurable. One teenage girl expressed it very succinctly. "I just wish I could hear one Christian adult say 'Sex is fun.'" Instead, what she heard was talk about the deeper meaning of the relationship—which she needed to hear—but never about the genuine enjoyment that a husband and wife can have experiencing each other's bodies.

In every Christian home, it is a good idea for teenagers and parents to draw up a covenant of premarital chastity which both parents and child sign. A covenant differs from a pledge or an agreement, either of which may require a response from only one side. An individual can pledge to do something for another individual without any correlated commitment from the other party. A covenant, however, requires commitment and activity from each side. The parent commits to a lifestyle of openness, honesty, and non-judgmentalism. The child commits to a lifestyle of willingness to deal with the questions of sexuality with integrity and honesty. If either one bails out, the covenant cannot provide the protection and the fulfillment for which it was designed.

The covenant should comprise an agreement between parent and child that the parents will be positive role models for sexual fidelity and that they will be open and honest in their discussion of sexuality with the children. At the same time, the teenager, being taught and recognizing that sexual expression is a good and gracious gift from God (but a gift that is to be exercised within the confines of a marriage relationship), agrees also to be open and honest with the parents in discussion of the pressures and the day-to-day difficulties he or she is facing. The parents, for their part, agree to approach all questions with an open mind and an uncondemning spirit, recognizing by their actions that what God has given to them in family must not be abrogated by judgments on the actions of another.

Preventive Medicine

Stepchildren have already seen one marriage fail. They have seen promises broken and a family torn apart. Parent and stepparent have now been given another opportunity by God to model for their children what a family is to be. An open and honest admission of failure goes a long way toward letting the child understand what a family can become.

At the same time, a repeated failure may cause that adolescent boy or girl to view marriage as "hopeless." A few years ago I saw a teenage television star as she was interviewed on a nightly news program. When asked about her future plans, she said, "Finish school, make more movies, get married." After a pause she continued, "And probably divorced. After all, everybody does."

In your family, God has given your stepchildren a second chance—the opportunity to see that a marriage really can work. Your actions will speak louder than your words ever will. You can talk about the sanctity of marriage all you want, but until your stepchildren see a commitment that you will stay by your spouse through thick and thin, through the good and the bad, those words will be very hollow. The greatest teacher of sexual morality and family values is the person who lives the life to which Christ called him or her—a life that recognizes the beauty and the joy of sexual expression and acknowledges that such a relationship can be genuinely fulfilled only within the covenant of a marriage.

CHAPTER
SEVENTEEN

To See the Big Picture:
To Be a Child of God

> The bond that links your true family is not
> one of blood but of respect and joy in each
> other's life.
>
> —Richard Bach

One contemporary writer selects the sandcastle as a metaphor appropriate for the stepfamily. It is well chosen, for the sandcastle's unsound foundation dooms it to erosion when pounded by the waves.

Likewise, for many people the stepfamily starts out as a hope for a new beginning, but because a firm foundation is never laid, the waves of travail (which every family faces) erode the castle of dreams, and the promise of the stepfamily is washed away. A man and a woman are left to face failure a second time, and the children's chance for permanency in relationship is destroyed.

Perhaps, in some cases, second marriages find the footing so treacherous because the partners enter into these unions less measuredly than they do a first marriage. Perhaps the second union is never seen as the ultimate lifelong commitment. The second marriage is called "second best"; the stepfamily, "second rate." And so it goes for society as a whole; the church largely ignores, society denigrates, and the courts regulate, seemingly without concern for those comprising the stepfamily.

No, this was not what your parents had planned for you. This was not your dream when you and your teenage friends envisioned the future. When we say "family," even we who are members of a stepfamily by and large think of a traditional nuclear family where children live with their biological parents. No, this was not what we had in mind.

But none of this in any way lessens the value, beauty, and necessity of the stepfamily. For millions of children, the stepfamily is the only family they will have. For many mothers and fathers, the second marriage provides them with companionship and a mate who will be an active partner in raising the children. For society, the stepfamily is a vehicle to combat the problems inherent in the single parent home. For the church, the stepfamily can be a partner in the redemption of the American home.

The God Who Provides

Perhaps we should remember that the God of Israel is called "the God who provides" (Gen. 22:14). As we read the Old Testament, we cannot help being struck by God's continual provision in his relationship with his people. Time and time again the people of Israel found themselves unable to maintain the context within which they related to their God. And, time and time again, God made new provision. When Adam and Eve fell in the Garden, God made new provisions for them and protected them in their life outside of Eden. When the

207

people of Israel were unable to become the nation of priests and to relate to God in a one-to-one manner, God provided the tribe of priests to make sacrifices before him. Even God's ultimate provision in the sacrifice of his Son was a response to humankind's fallenness and inability to live in the relationship.

In a like manner, God recognizes the value of the stepfamily and makes provision for it. I cannot help believing that God provides a special ministration of grace for stepfamilies. In the course of writing this book, I have encountered family after family with stories of how God used the relationship between stepparent and step-child not only to provide a secure Christian home, but also to minister to other families. Stepfamilies get a picture of reality that simply is not available to the traditional family. They see fallenness and brokenness in a way that a two-parent biological family can never see. And when they allow God to take the circumstances of their lives and use them for his own end, they not only find richness, fullness, and completeness in their relationships, but they also model Christ for the world.

In the Image of God

A church-sponsored movement known as monasticism sprang up in the early Middle Ages. The goal of the monastics was certainly worthwhile: to be imitators of Christ. They sought in all they did to create a lifestyle reflective of the one Jesus led when he walked the earth. Few could question their motives and, to a large extent, they lived lives of genuine purity and holiness. They were extremely devout and disciplined individuals. In fact, many of the devotional classics and writings on

Christian discipline which fill our church libraries came from the monks who peopled these monasteries.

Except for one area, the monastics led a life that could be exemplary for any Christian. Ultimately, however, that weakness caused the downfall of the monastic movement. For, you see, these monks practiced a private Christianity. Because of the evil they saw to be pervasive in the world, they cloistered themselves and withdrew from society so that they would not be contaminated. By so doing, however, they lost their impact on the world.

Many parents and stepparents want to practice a private discipleship. They do not exactly hide their faith, but neither do they give open and honest expression to it. And in their silence, they never offer their children the opportunity to see the impact that genuine Christianity can have on a life.

Scripture knows nothing of a private discipleship. Instead, the true believer is one who practices faith in the arena of life. He or she recognizes the evil that is part of the world's existence but understands that to shirk from that evil is to be unfaithful to Christ's commands. There is no such thing as silent discipleship. Either the discipleship will destroy the silence, or the silence will destroy the discipleship; they cannot coexist.

The biblical image of the family is one in which a mother and a father, recognizing providential interaction with the family, lead the family in a lifestyle of commitment and ministry. The imitation of Christ is sought, not in a cloistered retreat, but in the midst of the hustle and bustle of everyday life. Children see parents conscientiously seeking to be partners with God in redemption and diligently depending on his hand in their lives.

To model Christ for our children is to show them a lifestyle of peace and grace, giving constant evidence of the activity of God's spirit in our lives. When the stepfamily consciously and constantly recognizes that they are not only God's provision for broken families in a fallen world but also that God can use them as instruments of ministry, then our churches and our society will begin to recognize the importance of the stepfamily.

Seeing the Big Picture Yourself

One of the most important books in all of Christian literature was written by St. Augustine at the dawn of the Middle Ages. The greatness of this work, *The City of God*, comes from St. Augustine's ability to put questions and problems in the context of a larger picture. He saw isolated issues and asked specific questions, but he was not so focused on the individual events that he could not see the larger picture as a whole.

Those in the stepfamily, while not called upon to make a systematic response to all the problems of this world, can nonetheless learn from St. Augustine. Far too often, the stepfamily is a place where there is a celebration of the negative. Children bemoan that they are "not like other families." Parent and stepparent complain about interference from the children's other parent. The non-custodial parent finds fault with the size and use of the child's support check. For many stepfamilies, a constant course of complaints about the less-than-desirable situations that make up their lives has become their ritual of existence.

When the family begins to focus on what is wrong rather than what is right, the wise stepparent should step in with a new perspective—a perspective that sees the bigger picture. When the stepparent can accentuate the good about the stepfamily—the new relationships, the divine provision of care, and the contribution that the stepfamily makes to individuals and society as a whole—then those negatives can be swallowed up in the vision of what the stepfamily is and what the stepfamily can become.

To Be a Child of God

At times in any stepparent's life the need to gain the fresh perspective that comes from remembering our task presses itself upon us. We are called by God as surely as any minister who has ever stood before a church, as certainly as any missionary who penetrated the darkest jungles, and as clearly as any theologian who ever put pen to paper, to participate in God's grand plan of redemption. We are co-ministers with him, *not* rescuing our families from some imagined tragic existence, but joining with God to see that we all fulfill the design he has for every life.

There may be tears and trials, heartbreak and hardships. But there is also revelry and relationships, and love and laughter.

As you watch your children grow, when you see the triumphs and the tragedies that simply are a part of growing up, it is important to remember that God travels this road with us. Just as we do, God desires to see our children mature to become children of God. Our divinely appointed task is a divinely assisted task. Ultimately, he wants us to succeed as much as we want to.

SUGGESTIONS FOR FURTHER READING

Books for Adults

Ahrons, Constance R., and Roy H. Rodgers. *Divorced Families, Meeting the Challenge of Divorce and Remarriage.* New York: W. W. Norton, 1987.

Barnes, Dr. Robert. *You're Not My Daddy: Winning the Heart of Your Stepchild.* Dallas: Word, 1992.

Berman, Claire. *Making It as a Stepparent: New Roles/New Rules.* New York: Doubleday, 1986.

Brown, Dr. Beth E. *When You're Mom #2.* Ann Arbor: Vine, 1991.

Eckler, James D. *Step-By-Step Stepparenting.* Whitehall: Betterway Publishers, 1988.

Einstein, Elizabeth. *The Stepfamily: Living, Loving, and Learning.* New York: Macmillan, 1982.

Gruber, Ellen J. *Stepfamilies: A Guide to the Sources and Resources.* New York: Garland Publishing, 1986.

Juroe, David J., and Bonnie B. Juroe. *Successful Stepparenting.* Old Tappan: Fleming H. Revell, 1983.

Lorimer, Anne, and Philip Feldman. *Remarriage: A Guide for Singles, Couples, and Families.* Philadelphia: Running Press, 1980.

Messinger, Lillian. *Remarriage, a Family Affair.* New York: Plenum Press, 1984.

Schnell, Barry T. *The Child Support Survivor's Guide.* Salem: The Consumer Awareness Learning Laboratory, 1984.

Visher, Emily B., and John S. Visher. *How to Win as a Stepfamily.* New York: Red Dembner Enterprises, 1982.
————. *Old Loyalties, New Ties.* New York: Brunner/Mazel, 1988.

Ware, Cijii. *Sharing Parenthood After Divorce: An Enlightened Custody Guide for Mothers.* New York: Viking Press, 1982.

Wood, Britton, and Bobbye Wood. *Christian Families Growing Stronger.* Nashville: Convention Press, 1991.

Books for Children

Adler, C. S. *In Our House Scott Is My Brother.* New York: Macmillan, 1980. (Ages 10-15)

Berman, Claire. *What Am I Doing in a Stepfamily?* Secaucus: Lyle Stuart, 1982. Illustrated by Dick Wilson. (Ages 6-10)

Bradley, Buff. *Where Do I Belong? A Kid's Guide to Stepfamilies.* Reading: Addison-Wesley, 1982. (Ages 9-14)

Lingard, Joan. *Strangers in the House.* New York: Dutton, 1983. (Ages 13+)

Terris, S. *No Scarlet Ribbons.* New York: Farrar, Straus, Giroux, 1981. (Ages 13+)

Vigna, Judith. *She's Not My Real Mother.* Chicago: Albert Whitman and Company, 1980. (Ages 5-8)

Other Resources

Newsletters and Bulletins

Effective Parenting. American Guidance Service, Publishers Building, Circle Pines, MN 55014.

Focus on the Family Newsletter. Colorado Springs, CO 80995.

The Family Therapy Networker. 2334 Cedar Lane, Vienna, VA 22180.

Organizations

American Association for Marriage and Family Therapists, 225 Yale Avenue, Claremont, CA 91711. *Provides help in finding a therapist.*

Center for Parenting Studies, Wheelock College, 200 The Riverway, Boston, MA 02215. *Provides seminars and publications on parenting for professionals and parents.*

Family Resources/Referral Center, National Council on Family Relations, 1219 University Avenue, S.E., Minneapolis, MN 55414. *Offers guidance in finding assistance in your area.*

217

Family Service Association of America, 44 East 23rd Street, New York, NY 10010. *Provides guidance in finding the correct assistance in local areas.*

The Stepfamily Foundation, 333 West End Avenue, New York, NY 10023. *Provides information and research on stepfamilies.*

About the Author

David Z. Nowell received his Ph.D. in historical theology from Baylor University where he is an officer in university relations. David is also an ordained Baptist minister and lives with his wife, Susan, and two step-daughters, Jinnifer and Meredith, in Waco, Texas.